THE SYS TEM

BY JESPER ÅSTRÖM

Edited By Jim Ralley

THE
SYS
TEM

AUTHOR JESPER ÅSTRÖM, SWEDEN
EDITED BY JIM RALLEY, UNITED KINGDOM
COVER DESIGN BY MIKAEL ÅSTRÖM, UNITED STATES OF AMERICA
INLAY DESIGN BY SIMON ANNSOFIDOTTER, OH MY!, SWEDEN

TABLE OF CONTENT

THANK YOU

This is my first book and it is the first time I understand why writers always include this page. Most of you don't even read this page, as it is not intended for you, but rather, it is intended for those who were there for me, so that you could have the opportunity to read the rest of it.

MARIA ERIKSSON, without your coaching, I would have never started completing projects that I take on. Thus, your support is actually the main reason this book ever got finished. If it sucks, that's partly your fault as well. Actually, if you - the reader - believe that this book was a waste of money to buy (or bandwidth do download from a torrent site), contact Maria, she'll help you cope with it.

JIM RALLEY who edited this book also deserves mentioning. Besides being an awesome guy with interesting perspectives on almost everything, he is also a person of clarity. You know one of those people who can ask you one question, and it is as though you've dropped LSD with a new chemical composite, making it feel as though you just flushed your brain with the breath of an Ice bear? No? Well, that's because I wrote that sentence with my type of analogies and metaphors. As you'll read the rest of this book you'll notice the difference between the above sentence and the rest of the books' examples. That's Jim, making sense of what otherwise would have been impossible to read, understand or get around. Love you bro!

BJÖRN ALBERTS is the first person who read any part of the book and his feedback, although not completely incorporated in this first edition, was truly valuable for my motivation and for the final manuscript sent to Jim for edit.

On top of that I want to thank **JORDAN NASSER** who gave me the insight that I should aim at writing a specific word count every day, and see it as a treat to myself. And to Joakim Jansson who told me the thought process he went through when writing his book.

I also would like to thank **MY MOTHER** for being such an unpredictable person in my life when I was a child. Oh, you were there all the time, and I appreciate the hell out of you, since I would have been dead if that wouldn't have been the case. But given your unpredictable mood, I had to develop some serious behavioral analytics skills to know how I should behave in your surroundings. Without those closely nurtured skills, this book would have never been possible to write.

To my three brothers, **MIKAEL, JOHAN AND NIKLAS.** I'd just like to say that Tupac does still live and that our dead father is looking at the four of us from heaven, shaking his head, wondering why of all the million sperms, we were the one's who got there first. Also want to thank Jody who took the time to spar with me over messenger and gave me some hints as to how to move this project forward.

ALSO BIG THANKS to Lasse Björken, Helene Holm, Nalle, Agneta, Klas, Vanda Werner, Sara Öhman, Filip Dalhamn, Martin Roeck Hansen, Jonathan Gustavii, Lisa Walder, Tomas Adolfsson, Anders Sjöstedt, Thomas Björk, Katarina Pietrzak, Jonathan Briggs, Subhendu Mukherjee, Stefan Helgesson, Walter Naeslund, Sofia B Karlsson, Sofia Gullholm, Djamila Cardona, Annika Kreipke, Åsa Bohman, Thomas Backteman, Staffan Lindgren, Linus Gunnarsson, David Sandberg, Eleni, Kristina Bergwall, Linus Andersson for giving me the opportunities to learn all I needed to learn about these matters.

ALSO. Thank you to The Scorpions, Oscar Lavelid, Johan Malm, Johan Dertell and Diana Klugman and Kristian Grap for accepting me for who I am through all these years. Also, I cannot leave this book without a big up to, **TIFFANY LITVINE** for being the love of my life.

FEEDBACK ON FIRST CHAPTER

As a part of writing this book, I invited some of the people that I am connected to online to give me feedback. I promised them that they would be able to write whatever they wanted to. Some of them chose to opt in for the opportunity and so here are what they wrote. I told them I would publish whatever they wrote. And so here it is:

QUESTION:
What you want to write in "our" book :)?

MARYEM NASRI
Great learning! For anyone with products or services that people still don't know they need (hence, don't search for yet).

BJÖRN ALBERGS
Det bestämmer du själv :)

MARIA GESTER
This book will be a must have for all of us internet/marketing/nerds and geeks!

ONLINE RESOURCES
The reason I don't have any images in this book is because they would be limited by relevance and time. Instead I have created an online resource where I update images regularly. *All online resources associated with this book can be found here:*

The Value And Behaviors Of A Network

CHAPTER 1

GETTING YOUR BRAIN READY FOR THIS BOOK - WARM UP TIME!
First things first. You really need a basic understanding of how the internet works to get the most out of this book. But don't worry. I'm here for you. And it turns out that understanding the inner workings of the internet is a lot easier than you might think.

If we strip back the complexities and the platforms and the jargon, the internet consists of just three things: **content, people**, and the **links** between them. If you take nothing else from this book, please take these three basic principles. In its most simplified form, the internet is no more complex than that. The important thing is to understand how these three things define and influence how you work with the internet.

Think about it this way. If you have a lot of content, and a lot of people consuming that content, with lots of links connecting them, then you own a large proportion of the internet. The less content, people and links you have, the less of the internet you own. These are the key resources in the battlefield for internet domination. In other words, becoming a major player on the internet means acquiring as much content, people and links you can. This is what marketing, growth and online distribution is all about, and has been from the very beginning.

People often get confused when it comes to acquiring these three key resources. They tend to focus only on the latest methods and tools, leaving behind the ones that served them well in the past. The fear of being left behind is incredibly stressful for many people. In this constant search for the best and newest acquisition tools, they end up starting from a blank slate every time they come to create something. In the same spirit, plenty of brands throw away vast quantities of web assets after each campaign is complete, or when it comes to yet another redesign of their website in the race to keep up with the competition.

The addition of social media has only increased the importance of these three key resources: content, people and links. One could argue for the addition of two other resources that you also now have to manage and exploit: metadata and time. I believe these are both functions of how *relevant* your content and people are. **Metadata** is the way that content and people are defined by the platforms, websites, and companies on the web. Whilst **time** defines the 'best-before' date of your content, and therefore its relevance. Think about the masses of content produced and shared every day on social media. Social has made it impossible to be static. If you are static, you only serve to make something else more relevant. In this sense, the web is becoming more and more similar to the 'real world' - whatever that means now! - it that the latest version of something is more likely to be accurate than an older version. The internet, like the world, answers people's need for information.

Wow. I've packed a lot in there already, and I've barely scratched the surface of the internet and networks and content and the interplay between it all. The full story is a long one. But hey, if you ever get confused or have a question, the beauty of the internet means that as long as I'm still alive you can reach out and I can clarify. Ok? You can find my contact details at the front of the book.

So. Where were we? In short, there are several different methods of working with the internet in order to acquire more and more of those three key resources of content, people and links. As always, the devil is in the detail. In this case, the detail is those two other resources I mentioned: metadata and time. It's crucial to understand how they work and how you can play them, both in terms of people's expectations and in the ways that algorithms (computer programs whose job it is to find content and people and try to match the two) currently work.

This book will give you insight into one of these methodologies. The one I've been using, developing and perfecting for the last 10 years. I call it **The System**. It is based on a networking model where you harness a range of different media types to build as large a network as you possibly can. The idea being that the larger your network, the easier it will be be able to launch your next product, idea or marketing scheme.

The most fundamental element of my methodology is understanding human behavior. I start with humans as that is where my interest lies, and then I work to figure out how I can use my understanding to make people do stuff that is beneficial to me. This methodology works regardless of where you are on the internet: if you are working to make something visible in Google, if you want to trend on YouTube, or if you simply want more likes on your latest post. The methods also work if you are trying to transform your business, or if you are trying to launch a startup. Think of **The System** as a framework. Once you've understood how to influence people and work with their needs, then you can use your newly gained powers in whatever ways you want.

I will do my best to bring the methods and their application into every chapter. But really the purpose of this book is to explain my theory, and the application of it will happen out in the wild, on the internet. If you need more depth on a specific subject, or could use some tangible examples of a method, just ask me.

So. Here we go.

THE VALUE OF A NETWORK

I'll start out with one example of how to extract value from a network.. Do you know how to get on top of the search results in Google? Of course you do. But here is a short recap for those of you who don't put into a networking context for those of you who do.

Imagine you want to rank as the #1 result in Google for your product or business. Of course. Why wouldn't you? Nobody clicks past the first page anyway. You've tried loads of different marketing techniques, but you've realized, just like anyone else would, that organic search results are going to bring in the big bucks. Additionally, once you rank highly on Google, the traffic is virtually free too, meaning you will have *a marginal cost of traffic acquisition trending towards zero*. This might not make any sense to you because you are a marketer, not an accountant. But when you are trying to explain the value of organic marketing to your bosses - most of whom are business school morons - then I suggest going with the lingo that they understand.

Either way, when you're trying to rank #1 in Google, you need to have the right **content** to rank for the right keywords (the search phrases that people type into Google when they're looking for the thing you're selling) as well as having relevant **links** pointing to your website, through other **people** having recommended your content. In other words, as we already know, you need content, people and the links between them.

Google ranks people, publishers and online accounts by how much authority they have on the web. The more higher quality links you have pointing to you, the better you will rank in search results. This means that if a person, over time has consistently produced content in the same area that you want to rank for, then they have gained Google's trust in that area. If they now link to you, then some of that trust will be passed onto you.

It is like going into a room and asking everyone "who is the best at drawing?" If enough people point to Sara, you won't bother to ask the rest of them what they think. You will just go up to Sara and ask her who she thinks is good at drawing. If she says she's pretty good, you could ask her if she knows anyone else who is even better. If she says no, then you'll probably feel like you've hit the end of the road. You've found the best person at drawing. However, if Sara says yes and points to Karl. You will probably trust her recommendation over the recommendations of others. Karl is your man.

In terms of websites. If you are Google and you see that all of the websites in the world who produce content about 'red shoes' are linking to the same source about red shoes. Then you can assume that will be a pretty darn authoritarian red shoes page. This is how Google sees the web.

I don't know if that makes sense to you, but it does to me.

If you want to build a presence in Google and rank higher, according to this logic a good way to start is to get to know everyone who is writing about the stuff that you want to rank for. If you don't know them, then it's unlikely they'll link to you. Or, more precisely, if they don't know about you, and if they don't like you *or* what you do, then they will not link to you. The larger your network, the easier you will find it to get lots of these links. Then you will start to rank for a lot of things within your specific niche.

It's important to say here is that Google has moved its focus from giving importance to links from highly recommended generalist pages (like news websites) and nowadays gives more weight to consistent players with niche content. This can sometime mean that it is way more important to get links from small but consistent websites, than it is to get them from big and bulging websites that are about everything and nothing at the same time: sites like Buzzfeed. But we'll get back to Buzzfeed later and explain the purpose and use of that website!

IN SHORT: Links are good. The bigger your network, the easier it will be to get links.

But it doesn't stop there. The bigger your network, the easier it will be for you to understand what content people encounter when they're looking for a product like yours. Or more importantly, what would they search for, or what *do* they search for, when they are trying to solve the **need** your product solves?

This focus on needs is super important. Especially for new businesses, new products and for most startups. People have needs. They go on the internet and try to solve those needs. You need to figure out what they would search for, and what content you need to create, in order to rank for those keywords they are searching for, when they have the need that your product solves.

Think about it this way. If they already know about your product, then they will probably search for your brand name, or go to a comparison website, or ask a friend to recommend a few options and then chose the one which is cheapest. However, if they have a problem, or if a need appears in their life, and they don't know how to solve it yet. Then it would be good for *you* to rank as one of the top solutions when they search for a way to meet their unmet need. Right?

This kind of thinking comes easily to some people, and to others it requires some complex mental gymnastics. But it's important that you understand this concept. So re-read these paragraphs if you need to.

Solving unmet needs for people. I believe this is a good place to be at. Because I believe it is the only way of finding sustainable business growth. You're doing well when you grow because you meet someone's need, or because you solve a problem they have, or because you now do recipes for chocolate chip cookies and understand that people have a need for "a quick sweet recipe bake under 15 minutes" rather than an off-the-shelf Super Cookie Fudge Supreme".

Your product and brand is a commodity or a vessel to get their problem/need/ desire solved. Ok?

And so, if you have a large network, you will simply be able to ask them about their needs. They will reply and give you a full explanation of their needs (or as we will see later, 1% of them will reply), whilst another bunch will post to their Facebook-profile what they think about your brand and how it has enriched their very interesting lives (actually about 9% will do this), whilst the remaining people will simply wonder why you care, because they never have. They simply used your product or service cause you were simple and you came at a time when they were in need.

I will present two models (which I have borrowed) that will help you to ask people about their needs. The first one is great if you want to understand why someone is using the things you make, and therefore also what type of content you should be creating. The second one is really good at deriving needs you can use in order to prototype new content.

Now, you might think that I'm rambling on here without purpose, but without establishing the reason *why* you would use these methods, it becomes very difficult to follow along.

So. First, I would like you to sit down and think about your product, or mission or whatever the fuck you want to do. Then continue reading this book cover to cover and start rewriting your mission statement in terms of *where you want to be*:

WHAT IS YOUR BUSINESS OBJECTIVE?
How do you represent this business objective online? What will you

do in order to try and make this business objective happen online? Where is your content, who are your people, and what are the links pointing between the people and the content? (Oh, you don't know that yet... well gosh, let's see if we can help you to find out. Go to http://viralhack.com to find the latest tools.)

BUILDING A NETWORK - GETTING PEOPLE TO WORK FOR YOU

Now you understand the basics, and you get that *your network* is the most important thing you need to consider. Let's move on to discuss how you actually go about building and growing that network. I could fill this chapter with all kinds of retarded shit about how "people are fundamentally disposed to want to unite and gather behind a common purpose, and that we only need to give them the opportunity to do that." However, I will save that for later chapters.

This chapter will be far more rudimentary than that. I will focus on how to gather together the network that *you don't know you already have*, how you can start to think about it as a network, and then what you should add in order to make that network grow over time. Then I will show you how to interpret your network. How to figure out what kinds of people are in it and how can you best understand them without having to spend too much money or too many resources trying to segment them endlessly.

BIG BRANDS

If you are a big brand with a long history of digital campaigns, these principles will come in handy when you are trying to examine the size of your network.

Throughout your history you have more than likely created campaign websites, you have run promotions, you have even sometimes had people respond to surveys and possibly, even possibly allowed them to join some kind of loyalty program.

Everyone who has ever interacted with you is a part of your extended network. These are all the people who at one time or another found a reason to use your products to meet their needs. For them you were/are useful in some way. Either for the mere consumption of your product to meet their needs, or for helping them communicate some deeper truth about their identity to the world. Maybe you helped them to communicate the depth of their beauty and passion through the color red, and their friends in turn through the color blue, making them your perfect match.

You are a big brand so you most likely have one or more agencies working for you. You've maybe had a few (probably lots of) marketing managers, directors and VPs over the years. What you need to do now is to try and collect *all* of the assets from previous campaigns. That means all of the **content, people** and **links** that were produced when these campaigns took place. Remember, these are our key resources, and we need to start valuing them.

When you've gathered all of the resources you have together, you need to put all of the **people** into buckets of interest. Some will have liked the more entertainment-focused activations, some might have just bought your product, whilst others might be people who have returned to you several times since they were first activated (since they first engaged with you).

We're not going to worry about that last group just yet. The work you need to focus on now is figuring out the number of people you have engaged with before, who have stopped engaging with you. You need to understand why they stopped. Then you need to reactivate them.

Think about them as old friends who you haven't heard from in a long time. I think there needs to be a real mutual interest here. You need to have something in common with these friends. There needs to be a connection, and you actually have to care about the network in order to be able to reactivate it. But if the truth is that you don't care, then you simply need to be really good at pretending. Ok?

In other words, if you need something from your old friend but you don't really want them in your life. Then you need to come up with some kind of 'stop and go' scenario where you can activate them and then put them on hold until you activate them again. The crucial thing here is to always make them feel like they are getting some value every time you reach out to them. If they don't, they will pretty quickly figure out that you are using them, and then you're in a pile of shit.

So, at this point. Take a moment to reflect. Have a look at your agency list. Who might be sitting on an old email database? Who might know what happened to that popular campaign site that broke all of your records? What websites (and who was the editor of those websites) published your last YouTube video? Who put a link to your website in their blog last year? Who did it yesterday? Do you have this information collected? If not, I suggest you start asking for it. If you can't ask anyone else, then go on my Facebook page or to my website and ask me. I can give you some more hints on where to start looking.

However. You are probably in for a treat. If your brand has been around for a few years, I think you'll be surprised at the size of your network. Moreover, you will be *very* surprised at how many people will respond if you start reaching out to them. Perhaps you do that by telling them that you have just found a way to reach out to them, and that you're very thankful for their prior engagement, and that they are now on the top of your agenda. Hint, hint, hint... ;)

NEW BRANDS

For the newcomers out there, you have a bit more of a daunting task. Especially if you haven't got a single contact yet, or if your product is completely new, if it's like nothing else on the market, and is revolutionary and one of a kind.

However, if you're in the unenviable position of having a new product that is just like an older one - perhaps it's more expensive and performs much worse than older models, like the new MacBook Pro - then you're really in for some work. You've got some monkey dancing, lying and deception ahead of you.

But let's either hope or pretend that your product or idea will actually help someone improve their life. That it will meet people's needs in an effective and cost-effective way. Then your first task is to find your **first 100 supporters**. And when I say find them, I truly mean that you need to find them. You need to pick them out one by one and interact with them one by one. There's no way to shortcut this or do it faster. Without your first 100 supporters you will be fucked. Completely and utterly hand-fisted and rear-ended, prison style. From this day forwards actually, your job is to keep in touch with these 100 people every week.

That means you need to email, call, or text 20 people per day. Or about 2.5 people per hour. Could you do that pretty please?

15

Ok. Enough of me getting on your back. Let's put some "why" behind these demands.

I have come to realize that when I am in touch with 100 people who really have a deep need to use my product, I can get them to do remarkable things for me. How many times have you had 100 shares of a Facebook post? Most big brands rarely do. But for you, just starting out, you can create lovely, deep, meaningful relationships with people who will continuously share your stuff with their friends. In essence, these 100 people will reach about 10,000 people every time you ask them to post something. This means that you will have a reach of 3,650,000 eyeballs every year. And it's all for free right?!?

Nah. You have to put in the work. But it is more than worth it to get those 3.5 million eyeballs looking at your content (I make my calculations based on the average number of friends on Facebook, 300, and that about one third will share your message. I then multiply that by 365 days in a year - which is *really* not that likely, but we're trying to make a point here, so a bit of fudging doesn't do any harm as the numbers tend to add up).

If these 100 people each have their own website, you can give them a sample of your product and then ask them to write a review of how they found it, or why they liked it. You can nudge them to write that review on Amazon or in the App Store, or wherever it would make sense for you from a business perspective. Perhaps they could write a blog post about their review, or maybe link to their review from their own website. You have to focus on creating whatever content you need to connect with these people, so that they can connect that content with their networks. Using **content** and **links** is the best thing you can do at this point.

The next assignment is to get your 100 people to do assignments for you. Eventually they will each have about 100 people of their own that they 'manage'. We will get into the principles of **activation** in the next chapter, and explore what content you can produce in order to activate people in different ways. But for now you just need to understand the networked logic. You will have a network of 10,000 people in no time at all. What businesses have 10,000 customers? Really big ones right? And although you are only using your network in order to build a bigger network at this point in time. You will start seeing that your acquisition of network assets - **content, people, links** - will start increasing your rankings in the search engines, it will increase the number of people who use your content to connect with others, and it will increase your general presence online. You will grow, and as you grow and you focus on growing the network, then your sales or results (for example if you are trying to put pressure on a politician, your growth rate of people also wanting to put pressure on that politician will lead to the interest of journalists, who will then help you put the pressure on, etc.) will start pouring in.

It's important for me to say that this book will be a little bit like the economics course you took, or the physics book you read in school. Meaning that every chapter will add a new layer of complexity, making each previous chapter seem oversimplified or untrue. But hey, without the initial simplification and the initial success in your attempts to try this out, you would lose interest quite quickly.

My objective is to keep you reading, and to start to use these methodologies in your work.

So. For you newbies out there. I suggest you start with acquiring (getting them on your side and ready to share content) 3 people per day for 30 days. That's almost 90 people (because you will have a few lazy days where you do nothing at all, you're only human). You then make this your habit. Embed it into your daily routine. Contact 3 new people every day until you have 100 who are really interested in the stuff that you do. Then maintain these people for a while, listen to them, chat with them, find out what they want to hear more about, and more importantly take note of what they *don't* want to hear about.

If you are at the pre-MVP (minimum viable product) stage with your product then you should use this opportunity to prototype your product. However, if you are post-MVP and you have a real product or service that people can buy, then focus on those people in your network who have a clear unmet need. One that your product is trying to solve or meet.

This discipline has always been my magic juice, my secret sauce: contacting 3 people per day. Everyone else seems to focus on getting the big bang right from the beginning. Yet very few have the stamina to put in the hard work. So, by simply *following* this principle you will get linear growth for any product you want to launch.

But if and only if it meets a need. Yep! I will keep repeating that. It is *the essential element* of your marketing strategy.

Funnily enough, I heard a talk from a guy on Amazon monetization. His idea was that your first objective should be to work on getting 20 sales per day and 50 reviews in total. Until you have that you shouldn't try anything fancier, or focus on anything else other than just getting those 20 sales per day and 50 reviews in total.

I totally agree with him. When you are starting out small, you should focus on the most important things. In most cases these things are sales or the equivalent of sales. The equivalent of a sale might be a view or a visit if you are into marketing for marketing's sake (most agencies are), it might be influence over an influencer (in the case of getting a bill passed in congress) or it might be the download of a 'white paper' if you are in the B2B world.

Whilst we're on the subject. Why do we always talk about *downloading a white paper* when we talk about conversion for a B2B product? Can't we be more original than that? Are B2B people really so stuck up that they don't realize everyone is in the people to people (P2P) business, and that your success is dependent on how many **people** you can get to understand the usability of your product and what problem it might solve.

My second beef with the term 'white paper' is that it is called a 'white paper'! Most people really don't understand what it is, yet most B2B operators insist on using the call to action (CTA) "download the white paper on...". Can't we call the pink elephant what it is? A pink elephant. Instead of dancing around the subject why don't we just say: "I am trying to sell you on this idea that we are good, and this PDF is the best way I know to make you understand that." Or more simply: "This is a really useful document to convince your boss to buy our product." Or even just: "Really useful information."

It doesn't really matter what your opinion on white papers is. I'm just trying to reassure the B2B people reading this that you still have a reason to read on. Your sales, or equivalent (or moreover your conversion rate) are a derivative of your reputation, engagement, and online visible vanity metrics.

So. Let's spend some time on digging into those metrics!

KPIS, METRICS AND THE DIGITAL VALUE THEY REPRESENT

Have you ever heard someone talking about KPIs and not really understood what they're talking about? Well it's important that you have a basic understanding of what they are and how we can use them effectively for marketing. So here it goes. KPIs in this context, stands for 'Key Performance Indicators'. KPIs are used as a measurement of movement towards your goals. Used well, they tell you how you are performing at any given moment in time.

Good KPIs are therefore things that are easily measurable. Things like percentages or ratios or other mathematical measurements of change. Which ones are important to you, will depend on what it is that you are doing. But generally speaking, you will probably want to measure *how much* people are doing what you want them to do, in order to figure out how far you are from reaching your goals.

For the sake of marketing or reaching out, we have to put this into the context of our three most common silos (isolated systems, processes, or departments) when it comes to corporate structures: **marketing**, **PR / communications** and **sales**. Some organizations have different names for these, but their objective is likely to be the same.

Marketing has a challenge to *reach* as many people as possible. If they don't reach people then the business is screwed, and it doesn't matter how good the product they are trying to market really is. No one will hear the tree falling in the woods if no one is there to see it fall. So, if you are in the marketing department, your goal might be the *number of people* you reach. However, going beyond this, your true objective should be to *get people's attention*, as there is no point in reaching people with crappy stuff if they don't pay any attention to it. So, as a marketer your challenge is to get more reach, your objective is to create attention, and for me, the best way of measuring this is to look at engagement rates. Engagement rates can come in the form of the click-through rate, the view rate, or the sign-up rate. But I don't restrict myself to those measures. It should be any data point that measures how my content has made someone act in a specific way.

If I post one piece of content and my engagement rate goes up (however I have predefined 'up'), then I know that I am doing a better job than before, and I should probably continue down that path. If however, for some reason, the engagement rate goes down, I know I'm doing something worse than before, and should very quickly try to find out what that is, and try to change it.

Simply put, the more engaging my content is the more my reach increases in value. The more valuable my reach is, the less reach I need for each successful engagement. This only happens if I am constantly improving, and constantly doing a better job. It will save me money over time, and in the long run my marketing spend will trend towards zero. (OMG... not true entirely, but the way media spend is used today is a *big* waste of resources, so I will teach you how to use your media spend efficiently in a later chapter called **Bubble Transition**)

For the **PR / communications** department, the challenge is very different. The essential challenge of a comms team is to have a reason to speak in the first place. Which is hard for most companies. Because most of the time,we don't change our products, and thus our reason to speak is limited.

"Hey Mr/s Journalist person or vlogger! We have the same product or CSR initiative that we had last year. Please write about it!"

That doesn't normally work out very well. These departments rarely have a reason to speak, or to put it more brutally, they rarely give a good enough reason for anyone to listen to them. This means they need to either work on their business and update their product / mission statement / CSR initiative constantly, or find a way to repackage the same thing in a new way so that it seems interesting to the people they are trying to influence. Because, when we strip it back to its core, the main objective of the communications department is to influence people to talk about what they want them to talk about.

Now, one way you can measure your influence is to measure your **vanity metrics** and how much they have increased over time. Vanity metrics are big numbers that make you look cool, like views on YouTube or visits to a website. They definitely don't mean that you've accomplished anything except for a view or a visit. And remember that they can come from any place in the world, like Thailand or the Philippines and be easily generated by hackers using hacked printers. Even if they're not from hacked machines, these numbers are genuinely completely worthless, except in one instance. They can be really valuable if you use them *to tell others how hot you are right now.*

Imagine a scenario where you tell a publisher to put your latest commercial on their website. Naturally, they will object and ask you to pay whatever CPM fee they have associated with advertising on their website. Not such a great outcome.

Now imagine you could contact the same publisher and say that you have the most popular content on the internet, and that you will allow them to put it on their website if... They will now probably ask *you* how much, and you'll be able to charge *them* for your advert (not really, but they certainly wouldn't ask you to pay them, as their business model is built around the number of page loads they get and they LOVE it when they can get content for free that generates a lot of page loads). So if you have the most popular content on the internet, then you're in a good position to get them to publish it for free... in essence, you are scratching their back as they scratch yours.

If you have big vanity metrics (likes, views, reads) on an old piece of content, then you can also assume that the anticipation for your next piece of similar content will be huge, as people want to be the first to share your next big thing. People want to appear to be smart and cool. Just consider Apple, Red Bull and Volvo as three examples where they have done PR about how popular their campaigns became, and thus, increase the anticipation for their next act. For newbies and startups though, I'm afraid you really need some history to use this kind of tactic. Instead, remember that you're new and you're solving a problem or meeting a need for the first time. You have a natural reason to speak and you don't need to fake it to make it. You should forget the vanity metrics and pay close attention to the next few chapters.

If you really want to to get to the position where you can use your vanity metrics, you need a lot of them in a short period of time, to make sure that *your* stuff seems like it is the hottest stuff online. Once you've done that you simply need to contact people or make it publicly known through your 'about' page how people can use the content you have just published.

We will get into lots of ways to gain vanity metrics fast in the chapter on **Activation**, but you have to understand that unless you use them for the objective of influencing others, you're simply creating a lot of useless numbers that are essentially worthless. My bold opinion is that no one has ever bought anything because it has a lot of views on YouTube, but a popular YouTube video is much more likely to be shared by someone else to a potential buyer.

I won't elaborate any more on this right now. Basically, the bigger the number, the more people feel the urge to share. So if you don't have a reason to speak, then give people a reason to share, because they will think your stuff is worth being shared. And as I said, we'll get into the mechanics behind all this later on.

Finally, the **sales** department. Their challenge is, obviously, generating sales. Sales are purely dependent on the rate at which you manage to convert visitors of a website into buyers, downloaders, sign-ups etc. Conversion rates are dependent on many other factors than your page alone (which we will learn in the next chapter). Sometimes, your conversion rate to the final product, however, might not be the most profitable. Sometimes it is actually better to get someone to sign up to your newsletter *before* they decide to buy. An example of this is Obama's presidential campaign in 2008. They realized that people who signed up to their newsletter were more likely to give money several times, at a higher total donation amount, than people who simply donated right away. This led them to conclude that they should first try to make people convert into subscribers, before they converted them into donors.

Either way, your conversion rate is a function of your reputation. If a lot of people have talked about you online in a positive context, actually in any context, your conversion rate tends to be positively affected. So, in terms of increasing your conversion rate, a good measurement is to look at your reputation. The more reputation you have, the faster your conversion rate increases and the better you will convert people. The only exception to this is if you have a horrible media shit storm, which will definitely lead to a period of conversion rates close to zero. But don't worry, shit storms pass, and in their aftermath they leave a ton of links pointing to your website, giving you long term value, enabling you to rank for a lot of keywords you otherwise wouldn't have. Pretty dark right?! But that's the way the internet works.

As long as you keep to the "contact 3 new people per day" principle that we agreed on above, you should be able to heal the pain and mend your reputation over time. As long as you actually fix whatever caused the shit storm of course! And while we're on it, the best strategy to do this is to use your list of *most converting keywords* and figure out what negative results rank for those keywords. Then either contact the publisher of that website directly or have your network of 100 people go in and defend you in the comments sections.

Once the commotion has died down, after a few years you'll also be able to request a removal (if your name is included and the criticism is personal). Just Google "removal of old hurtful links from Google".

To sum it up. KPIs are key performance indicators that you can measure and track in order to figure out whether you are heading towards your goal or not. If you're in **marketing**, engagement is really important to measure; if you're in **PR / communications** then you should keep track of your vanity metrics; and if you're in **sales** then keep track of your overall reputation growth.

The funny thing is that as you gain either vanity metrics, engagement and/ or reputation, your other main KPIs tend to increase as well. My suggestion here is that you start out by doing more of what you're already best at. If you are really good at creating great content, then start with building engagement. If you have a really large email send list, then focus on building vanity metrics (as you can contact a lot of people and ask them to look at something for you.) If you really like hanging out in forums or have a loyal first 100 followers who are willing to do it for you (such as Redditors), you should probably begin with building your reputation.

Or as the Amazon monetizer guy said: "Your objective should be to get 20 sales per day and 50 reviews on your product page". Putting that in the light of what I just wrote, I think you understand why I like this idea.

HOW TO SEGMENT THE NETWORK YOU'RE BUILDING - OR, HOW TO INCREASE RELEVANCE AND RESULTS

There are many ways in which you can segment your network. In this book we will focus on driving growth for whatever *the thing* is that you want to get out into the world. For that purpose, I have found it useful to think of three main segment types to help me along the way.

The principle that my methodology is built on is quite old, and is not unique to this book whatsoever, however the way I use the behaviors, types, or personalities is, I think, pretty unique.

The principle is called the **1-9-90 model** and it's based around the central idea that of the 100% of people in your network, there are 1% who you communicate with who will want to *contribute to your purpose*; 9% who will want to comment and *have opinions about your purpose*; and 90% who will simply want to *consume your purpose* (by purpose I mean the need that you fulfill for consumers of your product).

In reality, what I have found is that this relationship holds true for the statement that: 1% of your network loves you so much that they are willing to do stuff for you without you having to really ask them or give them anything except for love in return; 9% are only willing to interact with you if they can gain something from it, like money, some kind of social status, or an artifact that speaks to the deep truth of who they are as a person; 90% however, simply want to consume your product or buy into your message, not because they don't find you useful, but because they are focused on having opinions about, or loving other things in their life.

Considering myself, I know that I am a 1% when it comes to digital tactics. Most of the stuff I write or make videos about are really long and complex pieces of content. I know that most people consume about 10% of what I produce (hopefully not with this book) and then form their opinion on me, or simply leave the content where it is. I am not a particularly fun or extrovert character online when it comes to explaining what I love, but I know I do it well for those who are interested. I am not a pop-tactics writer, but I try to get into the details and I take pride in doing things right.

The blood drains from most of my friends' faces when I start talking about digital tactics. They can't understand how this can be such an important topic in my life. They can't begin to understand how anyone could have spent 40,000 hours learning about this crap. At best, my friends understand the purpose of all this stuff, but wouldn't ever be willing to grasp it themselves. They want the 'CliffsNotes' version, which I'm not particularly good at writing when it comes to digital tactics or viral mechanics. It's the curse of depth of knowledge. I feel I know so much about it that there is no way to explain it all accurately (which in essence makes this book really really difficult to write). However, I know that if I write, there will be other people who will be able to shorten my content and turn it into pop-tactics for others to consume.

These are the 9%-ers of digital tactics. I am a 9%-er as well, but not for the stuff that I love, rather for the stuff that I love to be *associated* with, like politics. I love to have an opinion about politics. I rarely even question whether or not my opinions are factually accurate when it comes to politics. Nah, I just feel it, and I'm able to make beautiful political arguments that get people either love, hate or laugh at. I can make pop-politics quite easily.

With that said, I haven't been to a political meeting in ages. I haven't contributed to politics with an original idea since... perhaps never. I simply use politics as a means of communicating with others. I feel safe in these kinds of political discussions. They make me look like a champ in the groups of people who think just like I do. I also look like a threat to the people who *don't* think like I do.

I'm a 9%-er when it comes to soft drinks, frequent flyer miles and travel through South East Asia as well. I'm on fire when I'm discussing those topics with other people.

However, in most cases, for most topics, when we're not discussing digital tactics, soft drinks, frequent flyer miles or travel through South East Asia, I am a 90%-er. This means I don't consider those topics to be of any relevance to my existence, other than that I want the best experience or product that my money or time can buy. I am more than willing to act on the suggestion of someone else who is already opinionated about those things, and has figured out *the truth*, rather than wasting time seeking out my own truth.

Fashion is a perfect example. I am a typical 90%-er when it comes to the topic of fashion. Of course I do care what I look like to an extent, but I don't care *enough* to want to spend my time and brainpower on shaping trends or crafting my own opinions. Nah, that's the work of 1's and 9's. For fashion I'm more into just taking whatever is trendy right now and sticking that on my body. I'm happy to buy into whatever someone else tells me is the right thing to wear.

A few months back I looked down at the bottom of my jeans. I realised that at some point in time I had decided to fold the ends of my jean legs up so that the cuffs made a nice looking fold. Not a big deal right? But the problem was that I had NO IDEA why in the world I had done it. I had probably seen someone else do it, and then just did it myself. I guess I thought that was the way it was supposed to be.

The fold is genuinely impractical too as it collects dust and sand. So there is no logical reason for me to keep doing it. Yet I do. I'm a fashion 90.

Most of our choices in life are those of 90's. We don't have time to care about everything that we have to make choices about, so instead of making all of the choices ourselves, we depend on others to do it for us. We simply take what is socially or financially acceptable and behave that way, without thinking too much about it. Nobody is immune to this. Even the most opinionated people tend to have their interest focused in specific areas, and they just don't care about other things. If they're in a discussion and someone changes the topic to something they deem uninteresting, they tend to quickly change it back to something they want to discuss.

However, most of us, most of the time don't have an opinion at all.

This is difficult to take in for most people, as we desperately want to believe that we are smart and logical and lead a considered life. But think about it. Why do you buy the tea you do? Why did you select that specific tea from that specific brand? Did you really think it through, or was it just on the shelf in the store? Perhaps the store suggested you should buy it? Did you make a detour to buy that exact type of tea? Do you have a lot of opinions about how to prepare your tea? Some people do, but most people don't.

The same goes with the shirt you're wearing today, the covers you have on your bed, the tray you pick to get your food in the cafeteria, the parking lot you select when you go to the store, the clothes your partner wears, and the time it takes for the fastest of two elevators to reach the 12th floor. No. If you're not a 1 or a 9 when it comes to these things, then you will have no problem in letting someone else chose for you.

And so. When I work with digital tactics. I understand that I will be able to use about 1% of the people that I get in touch with to co-create my purpose (my reason for doing digital marketing in the first place), and I will be able to use 9% to translate my purpose into things that 90% of the others can follow. Regardless of what my purpose is.

Now. If you are one of those people thinking "well 1% sounds really small", then you must understand that 1% of 10,000 is 100, and if you're going to genuinely co-create an awesome campaign with 100 people across the internet, then you'd better have some darn good project management skills, I can tell you that!

What I mean by that (because after a bit of practice, and after reading this book, you will be able to co-create with much larger groups than 100) is that you will have no problem in starting out and getting help to co-create. And you will need that help. Because we live in a world where *new* content is produced every millisecond, and *great* content is produced at least once per minute. In order to market yourself and reach out through the mists of multi-channel communication, you will need a ton of prototypes. Nobody will EVER have the budget to beat a tight collaborative group of people who love what you do and are producing communications for you. Never.

Some stuck up creatives might disagree, but they are wrong. People who love you add something special to your communications: realness. If you can add *realness* to anything, then do it. Because the alternative is adding more fakeness, which is what you get from someone who isn't a genuine lover of your product.

Right. Let's get stuck into how you can use your 1's, 9's and 90's to make some real cash money!

HOW TO USE YOUR 1'S, 9'S AND 90'S

The easiest way to use your network is to focus on having your 1's work with **content creation**, your 9's work with **content distribution** (or commentary which leads to distribution) and your 90's should **consume** your content and feel the things that you want them to feel.

But what do we mean by 'content'? Any digital representation of your product is content in one form or another. It is whatever transmits the experience of your product from you, to your end user. Depending on who you are, the best way to conduct that transmission can take many different forms.

It is always interesting to me that most brands feel like they can only communicate their product, brand or idea in one way. Any deviation from that 'master plan' is generally frowned upon by the company who try desperately to cling on to implementing it. Or in other words, they say "don't fuck with our brand guidelines."

My only question is why?

Everyone learns new things and accesses new information in their own way. If our goal as marketers is to encourage as many people as possible accept our products, services and ideas into their world; to help them to understand how the things we make and sell can be useful to them. Then is it wise to only offer one point of entry through restrictive marketing practices?

Clearly I believe not, and that's why I always argue that businesses and organisations should include their 1's in content creation. They should work until they have a method to activate the people who are most engaged and knowledgeable. These guys love what you do. You don't need to worry about them intentionally trying to misrepresent you.

In fact I believe that the *only* way you will be able to reach new people and grow in the future, is if you allow others to translate what you want to communicate into their context. You need to learn how to communicate *through* people, rather than *to* people. Their experience of you not only needs to be worth sharing, but also translating into their context. We will get into this more when we discuss the **smallest acceptable truth** in the next chapter.

Legendary ad man David Ogilvy once said that your brand is "the sum of all the opinions about you that exist in the world". You need to be aware of what those opinions are. You need to communicate clearly with people. To explain to them in terms that they understand, exactly why they should use your product. If you ignore your 1's and take on that challenge all by yourself, then you will quickly be at a disadvantage to those brands who invite their 1's in.

If you're not happy with what people are saying about you, then that should be a sign that you need to change, rather than thinking you need to stop them from talking.

So I engage with my 1's to make it easier for them to create content around my brand. I give them tools and access to information, I encourage them by giving them praise (in private, as they are not in it for the fame) and I keep a dialogue with them through an easy form of communication. Most commonly I use e-mail or direct messages. I tend to spend about 1 hour per day, just talking to my 1's. Usually after lunch when my brain is in social mode and I can't really focus on other work. **The 9's** I treat in a completely different way. Remember, they're not in it to help me build something great, they're in it to build themselves. I don't know if you have friends like this in your life. Most of us do. Friends who *take* way more than they contribute, but who everyone still seems to love. When you tell these people about something extraordinary that *you* really love (you are a '1' in this scenario), they have a way of translating this to the rest of the group, making it seem as though they 'own the knowledge', even though they clearly don't have as much knowledge as you.

Brands have people like this who follow them. These guys will use a brand to communicate something about themselves to the world, and the brand is only useful to them as long as it serves that purpose. As an example, think about scientists, and the many 'pop-science' magazines that use headline facts and statistics from larger studies to build a click-friendly headline, whilst not really representing the study in depth. However, they are interesting, and the full science study is not. It's too niche. The magazines are sociable, whilst the scientist is complicated and confusing.

1's and 9's have an interesting relationship, in that they rarely like each other very much. The 1's believe that the 9's misrepresent the truth, whilst 9's think that the 1's are too focused on details. However, they are totally codependent on each other's work. The 1 is dependent on the 9 to translate their work to a crowd, which they normally struggle to reach; and the 9 is dependent on the nuance and fanaticism of the 1, in order to have anything to say at all.

9's connect the ideas of the 1's to the 90's. The more content that 1's produce, the more 9's will find it relevant to bring into their context, and thus the more 90's will be reached. For every 90 that is reached, some will eventually transform into 9's, whilst a few might even turn into 1's. Take the case of the scientists above: the article in the 'pop-science' magazine might inspire some people (9's) to talk about that topic at a dinner with great enthusiasm, whilst it might inspire others to get into that specific area of science at university to truly 'get to the bottom of things' (becoming a 1).

When I was working with Pepsi in the Nordics, we used this understanding of **the 1-9-90 model** to build a community of 75,000 people over two years. By the end we were having conversations with over 140 people every day, who we had identified as active 1's. They produced most of the content that we used to engage and activate the 9's, who in turn shared their experience with a growing number of people. Some people stayed with us for the full two years, whilst others changed their behavior along the duration of the program, switching between 1's, 9's, and 90's.

These tactics enabled us to build a fantastic amount of online equity - meaning that they gave us the ability to rank in Google, reach out with messaging about the characteristics of the drink's personality, and get a lot of views on our YouTube videos. All which were vanity metrics that helped us to engage the salesforce of Carlsberg (who owned the bottling license for Pepsi in the Nordics at the time) to sell more Pepsi. Which of course, was the ultimate goal.

In simple terms, we used online vanity metrics to create a stellar powerpoint presentation that empowered the salesforce to tell a new story about the popularity of Pepsi. Because of that popularity, it was clear to everyone that more Pepsi was going to be sold in the stores, which made store managers order more Pepsi, which made them put it on a better shelf, which made more people buy Pepsi. Simple!

When I worked in politics we used the 1's to produce blog posts about specific topics. We then used advertising systems to put those blog posts in front of influential commentators like journalists and bloggers (9's) who were really into that specific topic. These 9's then wrote about the topic that we'd pushed to them, thinking it was a trending topic (because it was just about everything they saw through native, custom audience based and direct ads). They were driven by fear, and the thought that if they didn't cover this topic they would be left behind as political commentators.

With them referencing the source content in their article, we gained tons of links to rank better for generic searches that voters might be making: things like 'facts about the environment' or 'abortion laws'. We were able to increase the traffic to the party website by 200% on an annual basis and 15% on a month by month basis, leading up to the election.

Every time I plan an event, or am part of a planning team, I make sure I engage with 1's who are really interested in the specific topic of the event. I get them to create 'pre-promotion content' in which they describe and explore an element of the topic they are really interested in. Usually I find these people online, in forums, or in blog communities like Medium. I ask them an open question, something like: "If you would add something to the current understanding of

X, then what would you write?" I give them a platform (usually some social network, or some kind of event website) to write about these things. I then invite 9's to either comment under the article or react on their own social media accounts. This way, I reach the people that they reach, through them. The pitch techniques I use to persuade them to engage with me will be covered in the next chapter, **Activation**.

When I worked with nation branding and promoting Sweden to the UK market, we (the brand) had to behave like 1's, mainly because we had limited time and no established network. We scraped the UK web for travel bloggers and contacted a whole load of them. We asked them what kind of resources they needed in order to write about Sweden. Their answers guided our content creation. As their replies came in we went out into the Swedish countryside to film beautiful pieces of bespoke content, documented them, put them on YouTube and re-pitched them to the bloggers. We had almost a 100% hit rate in the first round of seeding (which actually gave us problems in the second round of seeding as there were no more good blogs to pitch!)

Then there was the case of the soundtrack launch for the Kickstarter sensation 'Kung Fury'. We had engaged David Hasselhoff to do the soundtrack 'True Survivor' for the short film, and he had happily accepted. As this was a successful Kickstarter campaign to begin with, we had a group of backers to engage with and activate. Amongst this group were all of the 1's and 9's we needed (in fact, there were 17,000 of them). By simply utilizing their reach and ability to create content around the release of the soundtrack, we managed to get over 25 million views on YouTube, without spending a single Euro on marketing. As a reference point, the Star Wars franchise had a release on the same day as us and had spent $5million (I have heard) on YouTube advertising, gaining only 60 million views. Whilst at the same time, Hillary Clinton announced her presidential campaign and got a mere 7 million views.

We used the same principle that you're now hopefully becoming familiar with. Engage the 1's to create content, then pitch that to the 9's who will do the hard work of distributing that content. In this case we also did a lot of groundwork drawing specific niches out of stories - I call these **stories about the story** - which allowed the project to reach audiences outside of the hardcore 80's cop movie fans, who were the initial target group for the launch.

I promise you, that when you watch the video you will say "well of course it got 25 million views", but I can assure you that people weren't so confident before it launched. I mean, David Hasselhoff wasn't exactly the most sought after celebrity at the time, yet we got 1,100 publications to publish stories about his song release in just 48 hours. This is especially impressive as the film was a true nerd project with very little mainstream leverage outside of Sweden (where the movie's writer is from). But we still hit the viral jackpot. I believe one of the reasons for this hype was the way we managed to engage the *existing fans* of the movie to launch the soundtrack: the 1's and the 9's.

I've launched yoghurt in Japan, telco operator services in Sweden, done hostile takeovers of companies, launched conferences, SaaS products, and recruitment campaigns. Not all of them have been successful in the sense that they have brought down the internet, but a surprising amount of them have surpassed their initial goals, and through the engagement we built around each campaign or project, brands have reused those networks for future campaigns.

The **1-9-90 model** is a superb mental framework. It teaches you that there are different groups of people with different behaviors acting around your product, brand, or idea. Each of these behaviors have a different set of rewards and activations that will increase or decrease their engagement, and it's crucial to remember that if you only produce one type of content or activation, you will only engage one of the three behavioral groups.

There are many more nuances to these behaviors, but I tend to find that most people struggle to care about more than three. By creating content for these three types of users, creating incentives that reward their different needs, and understanding their buy-in and work ethic when it comes to talking about you: you WILL achieve consistent growth over time.

Oh yeah, rewards, that reminds me... I haven't told you much about how the three behaviors like to be rewarded.

1's simply want your love. They want you to care that they care. They feel rewarded when you give them updates, when you speak to them 1-on-1, or in groups where other passionate people hang out. Groups where they can feel normal in their geekery and abnormality. If you give them the time and space to be themselves, their love for you will grow deeper and deeper, and they will do almost anything you ask, as they believe they are doing it together *with you*. For them, your vision and mission are the most important aspects of your communication.

9's on the other hand will only hang around you for as long as you can make *other people love them*. Which for them, will translate into gaining financial benefit or social status. The perfect currency for exchange with 9's is access to information or scarce resources. Invitations to exclusive stuff, products, or events where other people of high status are invited. Access to knowledge that makes them feel superior in debates, access to systems that make them look more powerful (such as vanity metrics), or access to publishers where they can reach new crowds. If you have the power to give them the access that they want to be able to say something about themselves, you will make them shine. Then you will be in a position to use them for your own benefit.

Most of the time when I speak to brands, they want to reach out through influencers by paying them just like they would a normal publisher. That does work, but it gets extremely expensive in the long run. More worryingly, it can be highly damaging for your brand equity as you end up relying on communicating through people who will at some point have a stronger brand than you. Why else would you need them?

There are a lot of theories about brands not being in the same position as people online, and how they have much greater difficulty in building a following. This is simply not true. Most brands simply fail to behave like people, when they should. It's because of this that they're not able to get the same benefits as you do. Because you behave like a person. Because you're a person!

90's feel rewarded by simplicity and through deals. If they believe that they can get a deal or an easier life by using you, then they will. They don't care if you give them exclusive access to information or influencers, as your access doesn't give them anything tangible. They won't care if you tell them you love them, or if you shout about the vision for your company. They don't have the time to love you back. They love something else.

This brings me to another widely held misconception: that you can't use social media to sell stuff. I think it's nonsense. I believe that most people actually want you to provide them with offers. They want you to sell them good stuff at a good price. Most brands just haven't figured out how to embed their offers and sales as part of the social media user journey.

It is absolutely essential that you figure out a way to use platforms like Instagram, Facebook, YouTube, and blogs to engage your 1's and 9's so they can convey the usability of your products and services. You can then help these messages to reach out to other networks of 1's and 9's. That is how you create long term growth using this mental model.

That is also why it's important to segment your network using the model. If you do, I promise you will see a radical improvement in your growth and engagement.

The next bit of this chapter looks at how you research the needs of your network. This is super important in order to understand what kind of messaging you need to construct your content around. What do you have to say in order to engage your network? What do they need, and how do you find out?

FINDING YOUR NETWORK'S NEEDS

As I've mentioned before: if you don't have a thing that people find useful, then they won't use your thing. Or, they won't *naturally* use it. If you have a product that nobody actually finds useful (hopefully this isn't the case), then you'll have to work with marketing to *create* a need, and hack that need into people's heads.

That aggressive strategy often works, but it is a lot more resource-intensive. It is better instead to find the ways in which you can uncover the needs of your network, then work with those needs to prototype new content or products or tasks or missions or causes, that people already have a need for.

> *I work with three levels of need discovery in my networks:*
> Top level - values and inner needs
> Middle level - wants and wills
> Low level - preferences and timings

To help me extract these needs I use three different workshops that can be conducted online or in real-world focus groups.

For the top-level needs I use a workshop called **Jobs to be done (JTBD)**. I will explain the detail of the workshop later in book, and I will also maintain a page on my website with the latest videos and resources you can use if you'd like to run the workshop online.

The workshop is aimed at finding out *why* people really use your products, and services, and why they engage with you a brand.

Think about it. The reason someone buys a juice blender might not *only* be because they really like juice. Nah, a juice blender does a lot of other jobs for a person. It helps you to look like you're a healthy person when you post photos on Instagram. It helps you to feel less anxious about getting sick, as you can dose up on all those vitamins every morning. It might match the rest of your kitchen appliances so you look like a truly fashionable person. What the 'jobs to be done' theory supports is a method of interviewing people to uncover those inner needs, and find out what led them to use our products and services from the beginning.

For the mid-level needs I use a technique called **The ASK method**. This is a comprehensive theory of its own and I suggest you search for it on Google or YouTube to find out more. However, I use it is to figure out what people are *tired* of hearing about.

Most surveys focus on what people want. But that question actually might not be suitable if you really want to find out what they want. They often tell you what they think you think they want. And that is a whole different story. To avoid this, one of the techniques in the 'ASK method is based around asking people what they *don't* want.

The artform here is to hide the "what do you not want" question so that it follows the flow of the other questions you're asking. It should work as the reliever' or as an 'anything else you'd like to say' question, but be so direct that it gets right to the core of the person answering it. Put simply: it should help them to rant.

When a person is actively thinking about what they need, you don't ever get to an impassioned rant, because they are so focused on sounding smart and thinking about their future. This is a very difficult task to perform. You *do* get that rant when a person is focusing on what they don't like. That's when they let go and start typing away about all the stuff they really hate and would never buy again.

The way you decode their furious responses is by reading between the lines and looking at the words between the words. This means you should be looking for anything phrased like: "I am <u>tired</u> of my products always breaking when I really need them to fix <u>the X</u>."

How to unpick that example? First. Tired. What kind of feeling is that? What does it depend on? Why would someone say they're tired and not furious? Well, I know that whenever someone is feeling tired that they also feel, more often than not, helpless.

If someone feels helpless when using your product, or when they're trying to solve the problem that your product aims to solve, you need to think about how else you could relieve that feeling of helplessness. How could you improve the experience of your product by being there when the a user feels at their most tired and most helpless?

The second part of the example that is interesting is the phrase: "...really need them to fix the X." What is X? Was your product designed to be used to fix X? If not, then what types of products *could* you develop or how could you improve your product in order to better suit that usage? Perhaps there are other people who are using the product in the same way. Then you have a huge opportunity to create a new segment of products, targeting that specific, previously unknown need.

The ASK method is perfect when I want to figure out a user's needs, before I've been able to develop a specific product. Although the product they are reviewing in the focus group wasn't intended for this purpose, we all need a way in which we can point to a shiny object for a while, until we've sorted out the real problem with usability.

For the low-level needs I use a method called dayparting. The objective of this workshop is to find out *what* my users post on their online platforms and at *what time*. This gives me the insight I need to format my messaging effectively.

Adaptive messaging helps me immensely in lowering the friction to get someone to share something. If they are used to sharing a specific type of content at a specific time, and I give them that, then the friction is decreased to its minimum. Once you when they post, then you need to figure out if the content you want them to share is actually useful for them. Hopefully it is, because hopefully you've targeted this person because of their specific online behaviors. You're not one of those marketers who simply looks at how many followers someone has and then buys their reach, are you?

No. If you've made it this far then you're probably a person who understands that the only people who will naturally work with you, without you having to pay them, are those who truly find you useful.

I suggest you look through the 'Workshop' playlist on my YouTube channel to see some examples of ways in which you can find and practice this on your own. You can find it by searching for "jesper astrom youtube workshops" or by going to http:// youtube.com/c/jesperastrom

ABOUT THIS CHAPTER - SORT OF SUMMARY

So now we know how to assemble a network, we know a few ways to segment that network, and we know how we can use that segmented network for our own means. We also know how to discover the needs of a network so we can create products and services that they will actually buy and use.

Normally this takes a bit of time, and it is usually the part of every project that my clients never want to do. They want to get straight into next chapter, and start doing **activation**. However, if you haven't done this first bit, then the second part becomes exponentially - and I truly mean exponentially - more difficult.

QUESTION

Take a few minutes to reflect on this chapter.

- Where do you store your network?
- Who is in charge of your network?
- Do you know how to reward your network
  so that they will want to work with you again?
- What would you want your network to do?
- What would you measure as success?
- What digital assets do you think your network
  is suitable to collect?
- What's your overall objective of using your network
  and what other things could happen to your web assets
  if you got the maximum value out of your project?

"... you always have to begin with the end in mind, and work backwards from there."

How To Engage And Activate A Network

How To Engage And Activate A Network

CHAPTER 2

INTRODUCTION TO ACTIVATION

So you've put in the hard work and you've got your network now. You've segmented it into your 1's your 9's and your 90's, and you can see that it's growing at a rate of at least a few people per day. That doesn't sound very impressive, right? Maybe you want to speed up the process? Happily you're now in a great spot to move onto the next step: activating your network.

MAKING YOURSELF USEFUL AGAIN

You start by looking at the 1's you've gathered in your network. Take some time to think about what kind of content those 1's could produce that would excite your 9's. This content should excite them so much that *they themselves* feel the urge to voice their opinion about what it is that your brand does.

The thing is, that although you know what people need, and you (hopefully) have a product that meets that need, it is impossible to know what will actually activate people and get them to start engaging. You simply can't know this before you start trying. So you need to get yourself into an experimental mindset.

Now, in order to engage others, you need to develop a concept that will act as a starting point for them to create from. The concept needs to be **new**, it must be **engaging** (eliciting emotion) and something they can take away and **share with others**.

FINDING THE RIGHT CREATIVE CONCEPT

The first thing is to decide on the creative concept you are going to use. Whenever I've worked with online activation, it always helps to have a good core concept. It will help you to do less work, and you will see a much stronger impact from the work that you do.

The most important thing with the first creative concept or framework is that it should feel good deep down in your gut. Here, all the old rules of communications apply. The misconception around modern digital marketing is that you don't need a good creative concept to get results. That it's all about the tactics and the data. That is arguably true to a certain extent, as you can always optimize some crappy concept to get some degree of shareability. However, life, work and results will be soooooo much easier if you feel connected to your creative concept. If you really feel it in your gut.

So that's why I always prioritize teaming up with great creatives when I run a project or a campaign.

FROM CREATIVE CONCEPT TO TANGIBLE RESULTS

The second thing you need to do is to figure out how you can **activate** this creative concept. Now, when it comes to activation you always have to begin with the end in mind, and work backwards from there. For example, if you want someone to link to you, then your activation should lead them down that path. It should focus on getting them to do whatever it takes to link to you.

It's likely that they need to buy-into something (a movement, an idea, or a vision) before they do what you want them to do. Maybe you need them to do something difficult that requires a lot of time and effort. If so, then you should divide it into several steps. Starting with a simple task at first, then moving onto a more difficult task once they have completed the first one.

It's important to understand that more people will do what you ask them the second time, IF they have bought into the the reason behind why they did what you asked them the first time.

Remember your KPIs and goals here. Your goals are the end point that you're driving these people towards. Empathise with them. Think about the journey through the process you've designed. What's the last step? What do they need to do just before that? Can you simplify the process and reduce friction?

Once you've optimised the last step, move onto the previous step and repeat this thought process. What is this step? What do they need to do just before it? How can I simplify it?

This is the most useful way I have found to think about this, in order to connect every creative concept with the desired outcome of the campaign. And the truth is, that the better the creative, or the better the idea, the fewer the steps we need to take between concept and outcome.

This is perhaps why digital marketing is so much more fun than traditional marketing. You can actually design the steps that a user will have to take, to get them to do what you want them to do. Maybe you won't know this at first, but you can rest assured that with enough work, you'll find out eventually.

FINDING A FRAMEWORK TO MAKE IT EASIER FOR YOU

Now, this book would be completely useless if it wasn't for this chapter. I'm going to take you through a series of models that will help you to go from *having* a network to *activating* it, and sticking with that network until it does what you want it to do.

These frameworks are designed to help you unlock problems when you get stuck, or when you are trying to figure out what to do next, or when you're deciding what kind of activation you should come up with to make more people take the next step.

ACTIVATION MECHANICS - FINDING THE SMALLEST ACCEPTABLE TRUTH

We are introduced to new things all the time. Ideas, companies, products, movements, people. But there are only a few things that stick with us. Although my scientific basis for concluding this is very limited: I believe the things that stick with us are *the things we find useful*.

Think about a good story. When I hear a good story, I will be willing to share it with others if it pops into my head in a subsequent conversation. The usefulness of the story will depend on its character, its relevance, and the situation I am in. Perhaps I want to use it to seem knowledgeable, or funny. Either way, a good story is useful to me.

I believe that *usability* is of essential importance when we're working with content that is going to be shared between people. How can they use what you communicate to them, in communicating with others? What does it say about them as a person and what does it give them in return for sharing?

This is different for every situation, but I like to call that moment where usefulness is discovered: **the Smallest Acceptable Truth**.

I use the word *acceptable* because a truth (or reason for using a story) doesn't necessarily depend on its truthfulness or its factual accuracy. Rather, it just has to be comprehensible by the person using it, as well as acceptable in terms of their bias. If I want something to be true, it will be easier to accept it as true.

That is why I call it the **smallest acceptable truth**.

I use the smallest acceptable truth as a point in time where a prototype of a message becomes the truth, to explain what that message is trying to say.

I know that is a difficult sentence to understand. It's a complex concept. There is a linguistic term, 'synecdoche', that has similar connotations. But let me give you an example to explain what I mean.

When Facebook was launched, they had built a lot of functionality into the platform. There were the profile pages, the groups, the causes, the megaphone etc. A lot of different things that you could do and play around with. However, the only thing people really talked about was that you could find out anyone's relationship status. Anyone at all.

This was the magic juice that powered Facebook's growth. Other social platforms like Orkut, MySpace and Friendster didn't have this killer feature.

Facebook became 'relationship statuses', and that became the smallest acceptable truth about Facebook. When people talked about Facebook and shared it with their friends, they would say things like "you can go on Facebook to see if X person you know is dating someone."

Later, as Facebook opened up, they built even more functionality into the platform, and their competitors caught up with the relationship status feature. Facebook had to find another way of explaining what it was. How was it more useful than the other platforms? What was the new smallest acceptable truth? They built their whole messaging around another feature on the platform - being tagged in a photo. Think about it. They could have communicated all of the features they had. The event maps, the massive growth, how many people had been to your profile, the internal chat system. But no, they decided to build their notification system around the *truth* that 'you have been tagged in a photo on Facebook.'

I don't have the full in-depth story on why Facebook evolved in this way. But my best guess is that they noticed a lot of people were tagging each other. So they thought, "well hey, here is a feature people find useful, let's build our notification system around it". The shift was quite remarkable, and in doing so they found a new "smallest acceptable truth" or, in other words, they found a new way for users to communicate what Facebook was about, to each other.

Instead of having to communicate everything at once, they decided to communicate the one thing that was *the perceived truth* about the platform. As that truth pulled in more people, they could then design the funnel of discovery so that people got more and more engaged with the other features that Facebook had to offer.

I believe that the **smallest acceptable truth** is something very challenging for many brands. As most brands communicate, they want to communicate everything at once. Just go to a corporate website and you'll see what I mean. It's as though there's been an internal war fought about what should go on the front page. The problem being that nobody won the war, so everyone got a spot, and the page is a total mess.

This is a terrible way of doing communication online. The online format is sequential. You can tell a full story by approaching users with a message that they are likely to want to know more about, then you can move them from there to tell a story in a series of logical steps. Most brands don't think about this. They are still stuck in the billboard or TVC (TV ad) way of thinking where you have to tell the full story all at once.

That's also one of the reasons why brands have such difficulty working on Snapchat and Instagram. They have no understanding of how to build stories over time. They want to communicate everything at once.

A better way of communicating online is to work with your 1's. Inspire them to start creating content on top of your brand, using it as a platform to explore and play. Then just watch them. Look to see what messages start resonating with different kinds of users or fans of your product. When you find things that are generating discussion, you should grab them and put them in front of a few 9's to amplify their message. If the 9's react positively (if they do what you want them to do, or share in the way you want them to share) to the messaging, then you know you're onto something. You've found a new **smallest acceptable truth** to help you to communicate your message.

The smallest acceptable truth doesn't have to be the full story. It doesn't even have to be completely or even partially true. It simply has to be *acceptable* as the truth by the receiver of the message. How people receive the message, will greatly depend on what else they have going on in their life.

When I work with brands, one of the first things that I do is to help them work out *how* people are currently using their brand/product/idea, and how this can be translated into something that people can share.

I usually end up with a few alternatives to choose between. So I take all of them and run split tests using dark posts (meaning posts that don't show up on your feed unless you have been targeted) aimed at niche audiences. Whatever message gets the highest engagement rate, I select that and post it to all of my followers; usually on my landing pages and wherever else make sense.

If I'm working on developing a service, I try to look for the ways that users actually use my service. Either with tools where I can follow the full user journey (see a full list on the website) using a mouse tracker, or by looking at funnel flows in Google Analytics. Either way, I try to find what they like and how they found the things that they like in the first place.

Whatever you do, your goal should be to gain an understanding of what your users actually use, how they use it, and what they tell others about it. You could start by looking at your *most read* stories on a blog, or the specific element of functionality in your product that users return to the second time. The analysis should make sense for your company and your unique goals.

When you perform this analysis, you'll quite quickly uncover valuable insights into what your **smallest acceptable truth** is. Once you've found that. The golden ticket. You hold onto it, and amplify the hell out of it. You should make it your core tactical call to action, use it for notifications, social media posts or whatever other seamless communication you can perform, including landing page messaging. Measure engagement before the changes, and measure it after the changes.

How did the key performance indicators (KPIs, remember, from the previous chapter) change? Did more people share your content? Did they spend more time consuming it? Did they go on to take the actions you had set up as stepping stones towards your ultimate conversion goal? What happened? Did you find your smallest acceptable truth?

You might be wondering how you know if you've found it or not. Trust me, you'll know. When you've found it, whatever you are measuring will experience exponential growth for a while. There is nothing sweeter than when you hit this spot. If you're like me, you'll be watching Google Analytics, or any other real time analytics software, giggling hysterically away as your numbers go through the roof.

THE CONVERSION FORMULA

Once you have your **smallest acceptable truth**, people will find it *much* easier to understand why they should use your service, what they get from sharing your message, or how they can explain what you do to other people.

However, this is only one of the things you need to consider before actually getting a person to do what you want them to do. We call this baseline *Motivation*, and it is the strongest driver for people to convert. By convert, we mean going from the state of *not doing what you want them to do*, to subsequently *doing what you want them to do*.

So if **motivation** is only one, what are the other considerations that we need to take into account?

Well, as it turns out, there are 4 more. Depending on who you are and what you value as a digital marketer, you will weight them differently. However, motivation is the crucial one. If you don't get the motivation part right first, then the other 4 will only marginally change your metrics.

Actually, a friend of mine - Stefan Helgesson - gave me all of the considerations in neat formula which he calls 'the conversion formula.' Obviously! I've used this formula for many years now, developing ways that I can use it to build content for activation.

SO. WHAT IS THIS FORMULA? — $C = M + V + (I\text{-}F) - A$

C – denotes Conversion Rate

M – denotes Motivation

V – is the Value Proposition

I – is the Incentive

F – is the Friction

A – is the Anxiety

Get it yet? Haha... well, I didn't at first either. Don't worry, I'm going to explain each of the different components or considerations in depth.

Super scared by the mathematical look of it? Don't be. I'm here to hold your hand through it.

To begin with, you can see from the formula that there are three components $(M + V + I)$ that **add** to a person's willingness to convert. And there are two components $(\text{-} F - A)$ that **decrease** a person's willingness to convert.

MOTIVATION

Motivation is the foundation of the formula. It's your base, and it depends on factors that you can't really change in the short term. Manipulating motivation requires either a lot of effort over a long period of time, to *construct* a need in people then convert them; or (the easier and more noble way) you can *find* a true need that people have and work hard to meet it in some way with your product, idea, or message.

For example. If my need is to pee, I will initially be quite picky as to where I go. I'll probably look around for a restroom or cafe where I can relieve myself. Then, if there are no toilets, I will wait. I will wait until my motivation shifts from needing to go to a toilet for a pee, to just *needing to go pee*. Motivation comes naturally to me in the case of 'the need to pee', however, this also holds for consumer products.

Imagine I have a fully functional phone that I love. It meets my needs for functionality and aesthetics. Then imagine that the provider of this phone updates its software. It makes me annoyed because it's no longer the product that I bought and loved. It no longer meets my needs. So in this case my **motivation** might increase to want to try out a new phone. If I then accidentally drop my phone in the ocean and break it completely, well then my need and thus my motivation to get a new one increases dramatically. The two (need + motivation) put together, might mean that I am open and motivated to try out a completely new brand of phone.

Another operator might only have to give me a slightly better value proposition or incentive to buy their product, and I will be motivated enough to try something new.

Motivation also works in the sense of alignment. A good example is the American public, who *always* hate their President (no matter who it is) mid-term. It always seems as though the President will lose power in the next election. Then something always seems to happen just at the right time to reverse that sentiment. Often, with perfect timing the USA is challenged by some foreign threat. That foreign threat **motivates** people to rally around the symbolism and ideology of *America*, and consequently also their President.

Increasing motivation by finding an external threat works like a charm in politics and companies. There's something deep inside humans that makes us feel motivated to stick together in order not to perish.

Naturally, I have no scientific evidence for the statement about the USA above, but I like to use it as example as it helps people to understand what motivation is all about. Motivation is a powerful thing, and it doesn't necessarily constitute a part of a product or service offering. Our motivations change over time as our deeper needs shift within ourselves.

Many brands have been incredibly successful in using the power of motivation to encourage us to buy more things from them. The successful ones have built their brand over a long period of time, and have built up that motivation to buy. Their customers associate their own existence and identity with the brand, and the brand can charge them virtually anything.

So, in summary: **motivation** is something that comes from deep within, and builds on a need.

VALUE PROPOSITION

The Value proposition is the next component of the conversion formula. We define this as *the thing a person perceives they will get* when they convert at a specific time. It can be anything from a 2-for-1 offer (the value of cheapness) to a social status offer like "wear this, be cool" (the value of social capital).

A **value proposition** is a much easier thing to conceptually understand than a **motivation**, because we see them around us all the time. Usually a person or brand makes a proposition to a person: buy this / think this / do this. If the value of doing what has been requested is not evident from the beginning, the proposition is usually followed up with a counter explanation of 'why'. This is the value proposition.

Consider a dialogue between two friends. One calls the other and asks her to come along to a party that evening. The introverted friend says "why?" She instinctively can't see a reason why she would go. So her friend tries to convince her with several value propositions: "well, that girl you really like is going", or "there are free drinks" or perhaps even "there is this wide open space where you can sit and look into the distance... no one will disturb you, but you will look social."

All of which are compelling value propositions.

Clearer? I mean, in most western cultures you will be confronted by about two thousand value propositions per day. Just walking through a store you are bombarded with a series of discounted prices and offers that explain *what it is you get*, if you chose to buy.

INCENTIVE

The next component of the formula is incentive. This element helps a person to understand why they have to do something *now* rather than later. In my experience (both personal and professional) people are really keen on procrastinating and postponing their decisions. In order to counter this kind of behavior in my marketing messaging, I have to add a reason why someone has to convert now, instead of missing out if they do it later.

There are several ways of doing this. Normally, when we communicate a deal to an audience we put a clear time limit on every offer. Something blatant like: "this offer is only available for 24 hours" or "this deal is now or never".

This is also the general idea when trying to work with incentives. You should make sure that a user understands why they need to convert *now* rather than waiting. Depending on what industry you're working in, or what you are trying to make people convert to, you will probably need to explain this in different ways.

For high fashion, you can use things like 'limited edition'. If you sell seeds or grain or any other kind of bulk product, you can use a method called the 'dutch auction'. If you're trying to sell a political idea you could work with putting something in a setting where it seems like *if we don't act today, then the opportunity will be gone tomorrow*, or as in the case of the environment movement; "if we don't act today, it might be too late to save the planet."

ADDING M + V + I TOGETHER

Your task is to get better and better at adding the three components we've seen so far, together. The more you do that, the more you'll be able to convert people into buying your product, believing your idea, downloading your white paper (don't call it a white paper!), or grabbing your app from appstore.

NOW. TRY TO CONSTRUCT ONE OF THESE FOR YOURSELF.
- Take out a piece of paper and a pen
- Write down what you want other people to convert to (what you want them to buy or do)
- Now consider what might motivate them
- Then consider what they will get from converting
- Then consider why they have to do it now rather than later

Spend 15 minutes doing that on your own, and you'll have a decent starting point for your first conversion formula test.

SOME CONVERSION EXAMPLES

For my consulting business I conducted a fantastic 'Jobs to be Done' exercise which helped me to realize that there were several different motivations that led people to buy my services.

Find more on the workshop by visiting - https://goo.gl/YZX6PM

Only one of which was the fact that they actually needed the help I could offer through my practical consulting. This was initially pretty surprising to discover.

I found that they also thought I offered them security, honesty, passion and inspiration as well.

Those findings had a profound effect on me and my business. I figured out that I could use those new keywords when describing my offering to other potential buyers. My logic was, that if my current clients thought I was already doing a good job at providing security, honesty, passion and inspiration, then it's likely that I'm actually really good at solving those kind of needs. So I should start communicating them as part of my service.

In other words. I used the concepts of security, honesty, passion and inspiration as input to help me construct and understand why people and companies were motivated to hire me.

In terms of my **value proposition**, I looked at the kind of things people were searching through my website search bar, and what was trending in Google

Trends, as well as some keyword research tools. I could easily figure out what people's frustrations with their current agencies were by adding "don't", "not" and other similar negative modifiers: "marketing agency relationship *not* working."

It is a great thing to understand the baseline of the ASK-method, cause if you do, there are SO many ways of figuring out what people are tired of getting, then flip it into a value proposition.

More On The Ask-Method - https://goo.gl/YZX6PM

I realised that marketing managers all over the world were becoming obsessed with metrics, so I started to use phrases like "measurable outcome" and "data driven".

Then I added a 5-company limit as my Incentive component and the output was a proposition that built on a discrete and honest agency focusing on delivering traceable results to a select group of companies. It worked a hell lot better than doing the regular "buy consulting, here is what we've done for others", that so many other consultancies use.

There are 2 more components in this formula. So what do you need to know about Friction and Anxiety?

FRICTION

Friction is everything that removes ease and delight from a user's *experience* of converting, whilst **anxiety** is everything that removes a sense of *willingness* from your desire to convert. Identifying **friction** starts by looking at actual challenges that exist outside of the body, in the physical or digital interactions that a person makes along the journey to converting. Whilst **anxiety** is the same, but for everything that exists inside the body. All of the psychological perspectives that go into making a decision.

In the case of a website, friction might be things like slow load time, inaccessible forms, non-functioning buttons and poor navigation that inadvertently make people work hard to reach the conversion point.

ANXIETY

Anxiety, on the other hand, might be things like a lack of https (denoting a secure page) or 'verified symbols' on a checkout page, or photographs of your products that cannot be zoomed-in on, or no page with company information and no of terms of service. Anything that makes me question whether or not it is safe for me to convert.

In a social context, like if you want someone to share something to Facebook, then you have to consider all the anxieties that go into 'putting yourself out there' in front of your friends.

One classic example of this is Tinder. When the dating and hook-up app was launched, they asked users to connect with Facebook to sign up. As the use of Tinder was not yet as socially accepted as picking someone up in a bar, it created a huge anxiety that someone would find out about the Tinder usage. But Tinder was smart enough to anticipate this and added the clear message: "We don't post anything to Facebook" underneath the 'Login with Facebook' button.

MINIMIZING FRICTION AND ANXIETY

When you're working on minimizing frictions and anxieties you need to start by making assumptions about what they might be. Some frictions are easy to track and fix, like page load time, but many others are not quite as simple, and therefore more difficult to find and change.

So how do you go hunting for friction?

I've found that surveys aren't a very good tool to help figure out what frictions a person might encounter. People either tend to be too proud to say what they found difficult, or too shy to give useful feedback, or they feel obliged to mention things that really weren't obstacles to them at all, in order to appear useful.

As an alternative, you can try running eyetracking software or make Skype recordings of people using your website. If you go down this route, make sure you are able to see their face and their cursor movements. By correlating these two you can understand what is giving them a hard time on your site. Once you've figured that out , and you have a specific point of friction, you then need to dive into your own mind bank and try to figure out how you can solve that issue.

A third way of doing this is by looking at the time spent on specific pages of your website, then using a cursor tracking software (I've listed some on my website at https://goo.gl/rRnAAx) to find out where people hesitated and what made them hesitate.

Whatever you find through these methods (or others, try Googling it) it should give you the information you need to update your website, messaging on Facebook, or chat introductions. There are really only 3 things you can change: the design, the copy, or the CTAs. Once you've made some changes, you know what to do. Prototype, test, observe, learn, and prototype again. If your alternative version decreases the friction, go with that, but if it doesn't, try something else.

When testing for **anxieties** I've found that interviews or surveys are actually are very useful, unlike testing for **friction**. In fact, interviews are perhaps the only way that you can figure out what someone was actually feeling when they didn't convert. A good technique to use in order to dig deeper into the mind of another person, to uncover the truth, is to read back to them what they just told you. If they had constructed their answer (because of pride, obligation, or a desire to appear useful), they will inevitably feel uncomfortable, and will often start adding things or removing things or trying to clarify their position. It is then, that the true anxieties around your conversion path start emerging.

For example, imagine a person didn't sign up for a newsletter, and they start out by saying they didn't think they'd get anything out of what was proposed. What you would then do is to rephrase this answer in a way that makes it sound almost absurd: "So, you didn't want free advice that would have made you a millionaire". Then they will say: "Well, of course I do", and you'd ask, "Well, what made you not sign up?" And they would reply, honestly: "Well who would believe a claim like that?"

Now you've got them. They've revealed a fundamental trust issue with what you proposed. In order to fix or alleviate that trust issue you need to figure out a way to meet their need for *reassurance*. If I am faced with a trust issue, I always try to look for third party verification. Either through legacy consumer reviews or through association with trusted brands. This means, simply, that you should either put customer reviews or logos on your website.

If that doesn't work, and people are still anxious, you could try combining logos with a strong incentive to convert. You focus on telling them the story, that if they don't do what others have already done, then they risk missing out.

This is a practice commonly used in notorious Nigeria-letters. You know those letters that tell you that you have inherited a load of cash from some distant African relative, and the only thing you need to do in order to get the money, is to deposit 24 USD into an account. But you have to do it now, or the money risks getting lost forever.

The Nigeria-letters usually use a combination of a title, such as a lawyer or priest of some sort, combined with the incentive to do it *now*. And believe it or not, they are hugely successful. Although most people would tell you that they would never fall for such an outrageous trick, a sufficient number of people still do to make it worth the scammers' time.

OPPORTUNISTS VS CONSERVATIVES

Now that you've learned these concepts of **motivation**, **value proposition**, **incentive**, **friction** and **anxiety**, won't be able to stop seeing them everywhere. You'll think about them when you read any kind of commercial or political message, and ask yourself: "Really, they think they can get me to convert without telling me exactly what I get... pfff..." Or: "Damn, those guys really need to work on their trust artifacts for people to go with them... I mean, that font tells a completely different story than the message it is trying to convey".

What you will find, however, is that your new hobby can be very costly. It will turn you into a perfectionist. So as you start getting into it more and more, you also have to create a framework of generalizations for yourself. If you want to try to optimize every message for every person, you'll have to set automation processes (we'll talk about those later), but they take a hell of a lot of time to set up. It's much better, initially anyway, to start from a generalized perspective and then dig deeper and deeper once you've mastered the principles.

What do I mean by digging deeper? This is best explained by bringing in a new user segmenting tool: **conservatives vs opportunists**.

I figured this out working with a mobile operator. They had a belief that their consumer base was split between loyal and disloyal customers. The loyal consumer base didn't ever switch to other mobile operators, whilst the disloyal switched as soon as they got a better offer somewhere else.

I thought this was very weird, as it doesn't really make sense that almost half of their consumer base - millions of people - give such a damn about what mobile operator they have. I mean, they probably just want it to work, and as long as it works and they can afford it, they won't really be bothered. From what I've seen, only a very few consumers care enough about the quality of a product for that alone to be a reason to change. Most consumers simply don't care.

With this reasoning, describing the consumers who stay as *loyal*, and those who leave as *disloyal*, becomes a problem. Their messaging would be completely off if they ended up contacting people who don't care, with loyalty information telling them that *the company* cared.

All this got me thinking about conservatives vs. opportunists. I reckoned that the people who were described as disloyal, were actually active consumers who care, whilst those who didn't change providers, were actually the customers who didn't care at all.

The disloyal customers were **opportunists**, and the loyal ones were simply **conservatives**.

An opportunist will jump on a deal if it makes sense to them in terms of **motivation**, **value proposition** and **incentive**. They aren't scared of change, nor are they scared of the **friction** associated with change. All they're really interested in is finding the best deal.

Conservatives on the other hand, aren't interested in the latest stuff. They are looking for a simple, comfortable and **frictionless** living. They don't care about the best deal, but they do care about the one that is least troublesome.

So I took this new view of the client's consumer base and started using two different types of messaging. One which focused on motivation, value proposition and incentive which I marketed towards those people who I found were *opportunistic*; and another which focused on ease of change, stability, and other such anxiety and friction-focused words, towards the more *conservative* target group. (I defined who would be in which group by targeting older cellphones with the conservative messaging and newer cellphones with the opportunistic messaging)

What I found was that the conversion rates of the *opportunistic* target group didn't change that much, whilst the conversion rates for the *conservative* group skyrocketed. The reason being that we usually write offers to target opportunists, whilst we rarely write copy towards our more conservative target groups.

Conservative copy isn't much fun to write, and it doesn't sound particularly fantastic, but that's the whole point of it. In the eye of a conservative, *fantastic* looks difficult, different and too much work to learn. They are much more comfortable with explanations that say, "you'll basically get the same thing as you already have, but with a little bit more of the same."

What I'm trying to demonstrate with this example is that I found a way to cluster my users into personas, that I could then use in order to optimize my messaging in a de-averaged way. If I'd have optimized for every single user, it would have taken me too much time. Likewise, if I'd only optimized for the opportunists, then my results would have been much worse.

The key here is to find out how many personas you can afford to target, then use the conversion formula to calibrate what mix of **M+V+I-F-A** works for each specific group.

IMPORTANT TO NOTE: The ability to target a group is the most crucial element in this process. Even if you've identified a clear segment of your user base, if you can't easily target that segment, then you're wasting your time. So. Whenever I develop a hypothesis for a new target group, or whenever I see a new behavior that I can generalize from, my next step is always to figure out an intelligent way of targeting them.

In the case of **conservatives and opportunists,** I figured out that conservative people in general had old phones, whilst opportunists generally had new ones. It turned out that this was also true outside of the mobile operator world, and it worked for all of the other products and messages I worked with. So now, when I target ads or messages to only one of the groups, I make sure that I know the browser resolution of the newest and oldest phones, then target accordingly (this can be done with JavaScript on your website, and is a feature in Facebooks ads manager as well as Google Adwords.)

5CS OF VIRAL MARKETING

The first book I attempted to write shared the same name as this chapter. The idea was that it would take readers step by step through the five principles I use when I create viral mechanics in campaigns. As I was writing it I realized that my viral campaigns always do better if I have a network to activate. So I started my network research, which was the foundation for Chapter 1.

Well that book never happened, and this one did instead. Either way, you still get to learn about this awesome technique. The following five principles are based on the tens of thousands of hours of experience I have working with people in online environments. You can choose to use only one of these principles, or several of them in combination when working on your creative concept mechanics. By those mechanics, I mean the stuff you make that actually makes people do things when they have consumed your content.

THE FIVE PRINCIPLES ARE:
- Creativity
- Conformity
- Challenge
- Charisma
- Cheating

I've already posted videos about these 5 principles on YouTube. So in this chapter I'll try to give you a little bit more context around the human needs that are at the core of each one, and therefore also, the main reasons why they work.

But first a little story.

In the spring of 2015 I was approached by Universal who asked me to help them out with a project of theirs. They had bought the soundtrack and merchandise rights for a Swedish Kickstarter movie called 'Kung Fury'.

You heard a bit about this project in Chapter 1. I was bragging about how well we engaged and activated the 1's and 9's to get 25 million YouTube views and persuade 1,100 publications to publish stories about the soundtrack release in just 48 hours.

Here's a little more detail on the case.

Universal were eager to make this project a success, as the music industry at the time needed to move forward. Their traditional sales business had been decimated, and their revenue streams needed to be updated.

I was told that they wanted to create a soundtrack, and that they wanted a ton of views on YouTube for this soundtrack. For every million views they would receive a generous fee from Vevo (a video hosting service that uses YouTube as its main distribution channel).

I looked at the raw material.

'Kung Fury' is a short film about an 80s cop who travels back in time to kill Hitler. On his way back in time, something goes wrong and he's sent back to the viking age. There he meets up with Thor and some other ancient characters. He manages to get back to Hitler-time and fights the dictator in an epic final battle.

Naturally, that plot, along with the 80's style cinematography and VFX, broke the internet. When we took the project under our wings, about 15,000 people had backed to a whopping sum of over 600,000 USD. The soundtrack was going to be sung by David Hasselhoff, and the music video was going to be set in the same environment as the short film.

So. Our base network consisted of 15,000 people who had a vested interest in making this movie a success. Even if we only managed to activate them we would more than likely exceed the two million views goal that Universal had set for us.

However, the process was not completely without its challenges. And to be honest, I would have been quite disappointed if we'd just activated the backers, got the views, and the story had ended there. My goal was to use absolutely no media spend, activate the network the short film had built up, and get more than 10 million views. That would not only give us a nice bonus, but it would also be unprecedented in the history of the music industry.

As someone screamed at me before we got the project in the water: "Who in their right mind, actually takes an assignment from Universal to relaunch a D-list artist's (David Hasselhoff) music career, using a network of internet savvy peer-to-peer loving Kickstarter people, who have hated the music industry ever since Napster and the Pirate Bay trials?"

Well, truthfully, I hadn't thought about that. It felt like a challenging project, and that's all I really consider when I accept new project. So although this led to an anxiety-induced case of the fluid shits, I was still confident that we could create strong messaging that would shift the audience's focus from Universal making lots of money, to David Hasselhoff relaunching his career and the Kickstarter project kicking off.

We knew from research and from experience that people choose to believe in the most positive outcome for themselves if you give them the opportunity, whether or not that outcome it is the actual truth of the situation. So despite some anticipated cynicism online around the amount of money that Universal were going to make from this soundtrack launch, we would focus on the positive and kitsch elements of the project.

The launch tactics that we eventually decided upon combined a series of activation principles that I've already explored in this and other chapters. But before we dive into the full case study, I'll give you a little more theory around those **5 Cs of Viral Marketing**.

So let's get to it!

CREATIVITY – THE THEORY OF THE STORY ABOUT THE STORY

Has there ever been a day when you've managed to watched every single awesome video that's been uploaded to YouTube or Facebook or Twitter in the previous 24 hours?

If you answered that question with a 'yes', then you're not necessarily a liar. Your answer is dependent on your definition of *awesome*. As the volume of content uploaded to each of these the platforms increases every day, the insanely complex algorithms are trying their best to figure out what *you* think is awesome, so they can deliver more awesome content to you, and in turn you'll continue to use their platform.

This has created filter bubbles for us all. These filter bubbles sort your content before it gets to you, so you see less of the irrelevant things in your feed that the algorithm has decided you probably don't want to see. As an advertiser or marketer, as someone who wants to reach people, I have to be aware of this mechanic and adapt to it.

One of the best ways of doing this when it comes to building activating content around a creative concept, is to consider crafting a **story about the story**.

There are now so many great stories on large social platforms, we can't rely on having just one "story about our product", instead we need to break our grand creative concepts down into bits and pieces, each of which will become ultra-relevant for specific target groups. We need to let the algorithms know that our pizza video is not just about pizza, but that it has a super interesting and relevant story for every single ingredient, the special dough, the talented chef, the oven, etc.

The main story is simply not enough, as it only reaches the people who are already interested in us or in what we are planning to talk about. It will bounce around our filter bubble for a few days, but go no further.

By breaking the main story up into its components, we have the ability to reach far more people, to provide them with entry points into our main story that are genuinely super relevant to them.

Or in other words: creativity is not enough. We have to give the algorithms a reason to show our content to people based on how these algorithms work with *relevance*. The only way we can do this is by chopping them up into **stories about the story**.

Another way to think about the story about the story, is to think about traditional PR where you need an *angle* to make a journalist pick up your content. Every journalist is unique, and needs a slightly different angle to convince them.

Whenever I work with content online and want to build visibility in the mainstream press, I take a look at the people closest to me in my network and think about how I can activate them to get my vanity metrics as high as possible in the shortest time possible. Then I prepare a unique **story about the story** for every single one of the major publishers I want to get published in.

Then, when I contact journalists (who in most cases will behave like a 9) I can tell them that I have access to the fastest trending content on the internet. I no longer need to *ask* them to publish my ad. This is the difference between them asking me to pay them money, and them asking me how much I charge.

The sheer popularity of my content blinds them from my obviously sleazy PR tactics. They earn money from page views as their business model is based on selling ads. This is why publishers look at popular content like Gollum looks at the ring, with lust and greed.

The key thing you should be thinking about is creating *relevance*. Relevance is created by building a story about the story that gives publishers an entry point for the reader of their publication. So you really need to do your homework and understand what gets each publication excited.

I don't know if you ever saw the *'Epic Split'* video by Volvo on YouTube (watch it now if you haven't). That video was launched using these exact tactics. They bought their first few million views through a seeding network called BeOn. This gave them a ton of views in the first three days, enabling them to send a series of press releases saying: "This video of ours got 6million views in three days. Did you know that [insert **story about the story** depending on who's going to see it]."

They crafted lots of stories about the story to make this truck commercial (not the most exciting of subjects) relevant to everyone from the Wall Street Journal, to the Hollywood press, to individual users on Facebook.

The fact that Van Damme had done the epic split in three movies made it relevant to Hollywood and entertainment press. The interviews with the drivers made it relevant to the motor sections of the motor press. The trucks went backwards and not forwards which was of general interest. It was the first take that was used in the final cut of the ad Etc, etc, etc.

Remember. This was a video ad about the steering system in trucks made by Volvo. Considering the number of publishers who decided to publish stories about this story in their newspaper, I believe the launch process for this video is one of the most beautiful tactical creations of the internet era.

The video itself was beautifully made, but I don't think for one second that it would have 'gone viral' the way it did just because of its high production values. It needed the stories about the story attached to it. Neither do I believe that the publishers would have written about it if it didn't have the vanity metrics that came through the initial seeding.

In fact. When you look at the graph of views of the video, you can see that most of the views came in the first few days. Nowadays, a few years since its launch, the views aren't growing much at all, meaning that users don't naturally share the video. But during the activation period when all these stories about the stories were being pushed to the market, everyone understood what and why they should share. They had been made to understand.

I know what you're thinking. The video has close to 100 million views. It must be naturally viral. But hey, seriously. The video has been made to belong in the entertainment category, and in that category it is a highly viewed video, but it is still a baby compared to truly inherently viral videos.

The most viral ad (meaning that it was shared between users organically, and wasn't a product of an advanced launch mechanic) we have seen so far is the ad for Old Spice. They only used one story about the story that they seeded through radio. Do you remember which one it was?

It's such a part of the collective consciousness now that it's not easy to remember. But the story about the story was that *the video was shot in one take*. Go to YouTube, search for 'Old spice commercial original' and have a look at how fast it is still growing, as well being amazed by the fact that they shot it in one take.

There is one magic test you can do in order to check if your content has one or more stories about the story: it's the "Did you know that..." test.

Try to break your content down into all of the component pieces you can say "well, did you know that..." about.

Consider a conversation between two people. If they've both consumed the same piece of content and one asks the other about it, the conversation isn't going to go very far. Neither of them has anything to bring to the table to seem more interesting than the other person. So the conversation about that topic dies out quickly. There is simply nothing to talk about.

But if one of them had a reason to say "Well, did you know that [insert story about the story]" they would be able to keep the conversation going. Perhaps they have several stories about the story that they can use to keep the conversation going for long enough so that other people start to pay attention. As more and more people pay attention, the more people will comment, and become part of the discussion.

The more people who take part in the discussion, the more signals are sent to the algorithms on social media platforms that this discussion is popular. The more popular the discussion, the broader its relevance is, and so the algorithm decides to place the discussion into more people's feeds. Or in other words: the more conversation you can fuel with your stories about the story, the more visibility you will get for both people and algorithms. This will generate more links between the content and people who are talking about it, and in turn more links to your content across the internet.

CONFORMITY - WE ALL WANT TO BELONG

The next C of viral marketing is **Conformity**. This builds on a completely different set of human needs to Creativity. It focuses on the idea that we all need to belong.

The challenge with the internet, and with life outside the internet too, is that we are generally terrible at communicating emotions.

Think about it. How many times have you sent an "I'm ok" to someone, only to get an "Are you angry?" sent back to you?

The challenge, as always, is that it's just *difficult* to transmit your intentions and emotions to another person, unless you happen to be an excellent communicator, which most of us aren't. This challenge is amplified on the internet, as we are restricted to text, emoji, and sometimes video. In the real world, most of what we communicate is not through the words we say, but through the cadence of our voice, our physical posture, and a thousand other invisible signs that we're unaware of.

Despite our difficulties in communicating, we all have a need to belong. And people are willing to use whatever artifacts they can in order to make this job easier.

The need to belong isn't only a symptom of modern social pressures. As early as the 1950s a researcher called Asch did a test where he put ten people in a room. Nine of which he had prepped to deliberately give the wrong answer to a simple question about the length of some lines on a piece of paper.

Find example image and video on - https://goo.gl/YZX6PM

Which Comparison line is the same length as the Standard line? By looking at the model, the participants could of course see that it was line 2. But when Asch instructed the nine prepped people to say that the correct answer was 3. Inevitably the one non-prepped person went with along the group.

In the early days they credited this to irrational decisions in the face of extreme social pressure. But once researchers started using MRIs to look at the activity in the brain during decisions like this, they saw that it was actually the *rational* parts of the brain that went along with the group decision. Once the group decided it was 3, that became the right answer.

When I first heard about this phenomenon I concluded that I could probably use it to make people do really weird things, if they first saw that other people were doing them. I could manipulate people into making irrational choices that were extremely beneficial to me, rather than to themselves.

THESE ARE THE TWO KEY PRINCIPLES OF THIS CHAPTER:
- We are terrible communicators
- We tend to believe that the decisions
  of others are the most rational ones

I know that the research on this topic is highly debated. But for me that doesn't matter. If I get an idea, I'd rather go test it and see if I can find a case in which it works, rather than decide based on other people's tests. I know that's a very Trumpish thing to say, but it's not like I'm working with life and death issues most of the time. This is marketing.

I actually prefer working with things like fast moving consumer goods. A speciality of mine over the last few years has become 'edibles and drinkables'. I've worked with PepsiCo, CocaCola, Danone, and several of their sub-brands.

CONFORMITY CASE STUDY - OIKOS

The story I am about to tell you is of a product launch in Japan, where we used the **conformity** tactic to launch a new type of yoghurt for Danone.

So. Danone approached us for this yoghurt launch. The global concept was to launch using the image of the Greek gods.

However, all of us had a problem with this, and by us I mean the digital marketing pitch team.

The main problem was a glaring lack of connection between the desired action (switching from my current delicious yoghurt to this new one) and the image of the Greek gods. Why should I do what they are telling me to do? What positive association is there between Greek gods and yoghurt consumption in Japan? As we found out, there was none.

We decided that we'd much rather find new representations of divine influence. Ones that made sense for the new generation of people that Danone wanted us to reach.

That divine influence would be driven by **conformity**.

We wanted to train people into thinking that by using this yoghurt, they belonged to *the group of people who ate this yoghurt*. We wanted to train them into believing that if they ate any other brand of yoghurt, they would be outsiders.

In order to do this, we needed to set a pretext for some kind of *sense of belonging* associated with our yoghurt.

Exactly what the meaning of this pretext was, didn't really matter to us, as it wouldn't ultimately matter. Our only objective was to get as many people as possible to say that they were part of this yoghurt gang, so that more people would believe they had to use this yoghurt in order to say that *they* were now a part of the yoghurt gang.

Got it?!

Building on the powerful idea of **conformity**, our job was to figure out a way to build the perception in people's minds that they could use this yoghurt to say something about themselves. The theory of filter bubbles told us that we needed multiple messages to make this relevant to multiple bubbles, and thus reach more people.

So, how did we go about doing this?

In short, we exchanged the Greek gods with real Japanese youth gods. Which we defined as mid-tier Instagrammers. Since we (and Danone) had no network to spread this new yoghurt through, as it was new, we needed to tap into theirs.

The idea was to get the Instagrammers to come up with a story based on the basic brief: *You do work, you get hungry, you get satisfied by Oikos.*

Prior to sending them the brief we'd also done some research on their Instagram accounts, and found that they didn't have any professional-looking video on their channels.

Now to connect this case study to the **conversion formula**.

If you think about how I described the conversion formula above, these three steps we took to working with the Instagrammers removed the potential **friction** and **anxiety** that would otherwise have been associated with branded content in the minds of potential consumers.

We offered professional video content, which made the Instagrammers look like superstars. This increased both **motivation** and the **value proposition**, as their main currency with their fans is fame. The choice of high quality video as a format made it easy for them to slip it into their own narrative, and to not alienate their own fans. So **anxiety** was reduced. And as we were the ones producing the actual content, they experienced very little **friction** in terms of time it took to engage with the collaboration.

This is how you need to start thinking if you want to get your 9's to post your content. Because of our focus on increasing **M+V** and reducing **-A-F**, we only had to pay the Instagrammers a very modest fee. If we hadn't done it this way, then we would have needed a much higher budget.

Every time you need someone to convert to a behavior that you want, you should try to apply the conversion formula. Use it to figure out what might motivate that person to help you out.

PAYING THEM WITH VANITY

So, once we'd got them to accept the deal, we needed to find a way to reward them publicly. In this case the currency was self-evident, as most Instagrammers live and die by the number of *likes* they receive.

So our objective became to build a launch tactic where they would receive more likes, shares and comments then they usually do, when they posted the Oikos-material.

The solution was a mix between traditional campaign website thinking and modern spam philosophies. Or in simpler terms: we built a campaign website that included their posts from Instagram.

Now we needed people to discover this website so we bought cheap, lazy traffic, from platforms and audiences that we know are always out looking for entertainment.

We then led that traffic on to the campaign website where they could easily view and *like* the content pulled from Instagram. As it was the only activity available on this platform, the conversion rate from *visit* to *like* was quite satisfactory to say the least!

So we had our story. We could now say to our influencers that: "If you post Oikos videos, you will be highly rewarded by your followers".

SETTING THE BEHAVIOR

All we needed now was for the followers of the influencers to start acting like copycats. We prepared and executed this tactic to a similar level of detail, but we also got lucky.

One of the instagrammers we were working with got a response from one of her fans about Okios, and ended up forwarding that to her followers.

This triggered a chain reaction, as everyone who saw this also wanted to get a mention from this Instagram demi-god. So they went out, bought their own Oikos, and selfied like crazy.

The domino effect took hold. The followers of the followers saw these guys posting photos of yoghurt and the hashtags they used. Perhaps they understood why these guys were using Oikos in their photos, perhaps not. The point is, that once you've created a behavior pattern between a 9 and their followers (their 9's!), people will follow. People want to belong to the group. They want to **conform**.

In this case, we'd clearly designed the product into the mass participation mechanic, and sales increased.

THE CASE

The Oikos launch is a typical situation where you can use the mechanics of human biases to build a behavior that is beneficial to your cause.

In our case we were challenged to figure out what would make the influencers convert within our limited budget. We made some assumptions about what we could make their followers do, and how this would be perceived by the influencers. We caught a break with some lucky social reposting (which you generally always will, and in fact if you want that *lucky break* enough, keep changing what you do until it happens, and then it looks like you've planned for it!), and took that lucky opportunity to build PR around the case. So we ended up building on the popularity and velocity of the user-generated portions of the campaign.

CHALLENGE

The third principle of viral marketing is that of the **challenge**. This is probably the most natural state for the viral mechanic, as it takes at least 'two to tango' in a challenge scenario. Virality is therefore built into a challenge. Actually, if you're doing things right, all challenges should be 'viral' to a certain degree.

There are some great examples of viral challenges from the past few years, and when analyzing what they have in common I've come up with two simple rules:

- Place limitations on the *number of people* challenged
- Place limitations on the *time* you can respond

LIMITATIONS ON PEOPLE

The value of scarcity is deeply ingrained inside the minds of humans. I don't know why, but it's there, and it's a powerful force to tap into. This is evident to the extent that if you create a challenge where people can challenge *anyone*, you will actually get less participants than if you limit it to them being able to challenge just *a few people*.

CONSIDER THE TWO FOLLOWING STATEMENTS:
"Challenge anyone to a fight to the death."
AND…
"Challenge your worst enemy to a fight to the death."

Taking the rule I stated above into account, which one would see the most challenges completed?

Obviously the second one, right? And for two important reasons. First is that it feels more meaningful to send a challenge to the person I consider to be my worst enemy. Second is that *my enemy* then receives a highly personalised response, and will be triggered to act. It's so much more powerful to receive a personal attack than to be 1 of 100 people.

So the recipient feels more important and they will be more likely to complete the challenge. The completion generates a feeling of achievement in both participants, and they are more likely to repeat the challenge. This in turn helps it to reach more people, growing at a rapid pace for each new participant that joins.

Limitations on time

The second key to viral success when it comes to **challenges** is to limit the time in which a recipient can respond. If you remember back to the **incentive** variable from the conversion model you will understand the underlying mechanic here. If not, just skip back and re-read that section.

The idea here is to send something where the recipient understands that they will lose the opportunity to respond if they don't respond right away.

> **CONSIDER THESE TWO STATEMENTS:**
> "Challenge your worst enemy to a fight to the death."
> **AND...**
> "Challenge your worst enemy to a fight to the death. If they don't strike back in 3 hours, you will win an epic victory!"

> **THEN CONSIDER THE MESSAGING TO THE RECIPIENT:**
> "Person X has challenged you to a fight to the death. If you don't respond within 3 hours, you will lose a shameful death!"

I challenge you to create a challenge for one of your colleagues. Studies show that if you don't practice things you learn within a day, you risk losing that hard-earned knowledge forever!

(Not a joke. Your time to practice. Go ahead and send a challenge mail to a colleague right away.)

CHARISMA

Charisma is the viral principle that builds on the need that some people have to stand out in a crowd. Not everyone has this need, and it's crucial to figure out *when* and *how* to use this principle most effectively. Startups often use it, although most of them get it wrong. In fact, almost everyone gets it wrong in both the detail and the execution.

The principle builds on the scarcity of a specific resource. You give a limited number of people access to that resource. But you don't settle for just giving them access, you also give them the ability to grant access to a limited number of *other* people.

Most startups use this mechanic to create their invitation systems. However, they almost always fail to fully set up the play, before they put it into motion.

What I mean by that, is that they create a fully functioning and technically excellent referral system, without spending any time at all on researching things like **motivations** and **value propositions**. The things they need to make charismatic people (such as influencers) care about their launch and their product.

If you want the **charisma** principle to work for you, then you have to start by building a sense of *scarcity* around the invite that you want people to accept.

The way to do this is to use a combo of data scraping and PR.

Scrape the most popular blogs, Instagram accounts and journalist publications that the people you wish to reach out through engage with on a regular basis. Look for popular phrases, themes, etc, that fit your product.
Now create a **story about the story** that fits whatever is trending right now (think about the **creativity** principle from above) and frame your invite within that story about the story.

Pitch your story about the story to the blogs, Instagrammers and journalists, adding the perspective of the scarcity that you want to plant.
Pitch pitch pitch until you get published, or buy anonymous editorial placement somewhere (if you still really suck at pitching, find out how you can do this after you've read the **Seeding** chapter)
Now grab your list of people you want to reach out through and send them a link to the story, telling them that they are one of the selected few mentioned in the article (and making sure that they are).

This used to work beautifully. However, nowadays basically all startups are doing this, and the response rates have plummeted. So you need to add three more steps in order to make your invite irresistible, and to make activation inevitable:

Once you realize that the influencer you want to reach out through hasn't redeemed their invite, send another email with the subject line "Cancellation notice - 1 day left". In the email describe how they will lose their "exclusive invite" if they don't redeem it within 24 hours. You'll hopefully notice the powerful effect that trying to take something away from someone has, as opposed to giving them something they didn't ask for.

The second step is to *always* make them wait before they can actually start using your service. If a person is given access right away they will be busy using your service, and have much less time to write invite messages to the people you want to reach through them. So make sure you implement some kind of waiting period between redeeming the invite and them actually being able to use the service. It can be anything from a "validation period" to a "since you didn't redeem your first invite, we need to check..."

The third step is to create a page where you pre-write invitation text that the influencer can use while they wait.

If you want to be aggressive you can add an incentive to them sharing. Something like "secure your place" or "jump the waitlist" or "people are joining, do you want to be the person who invited them first?"

With most top tier influencers I would discourage the use of copy like that, as they need to feel pampered, not used. Instead use phrases like "check-out your invites at your own convenience" or "to improve your experience of our app, get at least one friend to join with one of your invites, and use it together."

The pioneers of this tactic were Gmail, Spotify and Facebook. Although they were the first, they will surely not be the last. I use this tactic whenever I have an event that I want people to come to.

I pay one or two people (or write a guest post if it is a more professional event) to post something about the event on their blogs or Instagram. Then I advertise that article to custom audiences on social networks that contain the people who I want to go to the event. By doing this I am raising the exclusivity and scarcity of the event (I will go through more of those tactics in a later chapter about **Bubble Transition**).

Then I create the invite and send it to the list of people I want to join my event. I do this both when I charge for the tickets and when they are free for the influencers. I use **incentive** copy wherever needed to push people to convert now rather than later.

CHEATING

The principle of **cheating** is all about making something look more popular than it is. If you remember the **anxiety** variable from the conversion formula, you also perhaps remember that people are scared about making the wrong decisions.

By tricking people into thinking that something is popular (especially when you're targeting the 90% of consumers who don't feel they have the time to research you), you can make people share your stuff simply because it looks popular.

I mean, this is nothing new to us. When the popular kid in school started wearing that new pair of sneakers, everyone followed. Everyone except for us poor kids who didn't have the money. We had to fake it by getting the cheap variant of the same shoe, then pimp it so it looked like the more expensive kind.

The representation of these poor kids in the digital world, is when companies or people use likes, views, followers and other vanity metrics to seem more popular than they really are. Making their followers believe that they've earned it. So following this person goes from being something you can choose, into something that is a necessity. What if you miss out on that next video or photo that everyone will definitely be talking about? You will look like a fool.

It's interesting to think about the extent of what we're willing to believe, as long as we believe what we believe is the majority belief.

To give you an example of this, I'm going to take you a few years back in time to when the blogosphere started growing in Sweden. A toplist of the most popular blogs was created on a website called 'blogportal'. The way you ranked on the toplist was by installing their script on your site, which then measured the number of visitors you had.

Back then Google Analytics and other measurement tools weren't as dominant, and so, for many people, this was the only way of knowing how many visitors you had on your blog. It became a sign of status.

If you had a lot of traffic, you had a lot of influence. Or... that was the general idea.

What most people didn't know at the time, was that many of the top 100 bloggers on the list belonged to the same network. They were backed by a group of guys who were incredibly internet-savvy and had decided to 'help' their bloggers out by buying spam traffic to these websites.

Since the script from the blog portal wasn't able to distinguish between real traffic and spam traffic, the bloggers who used this method climbed the charts faster than a rabbit fucks.

They quickly outranked many of the other blogs in the Swedish market who hadn't used the spamming method.

Consequently, people developed the opinion that the content on the spammed blogs was great, because it was popular. Because why would something that is popular be of poor quality?

This had some interesting side effects. People who went on the toplist couldn't figure out why some of the most popular content was total garbage. Instead of discarding these blogs, or questioned the quality of the content on them, they questioned *themselves*. They believed that the toplist contained the truth. *They* must have been the problem.

This set a precedent which took many years to correct in the Swedish blogosphere. In most other countries a rich flora of different of blogs grew huge followings, and a variety of different views on the world were shared. In Sweden however, the definition of what a blogger was, became extremely homogeneous, and at times the profession was frowned upon as something of superficial and of low quality.

This belief hurt the Swedish blogging community. You couldn't be taken seriously if you had written something in a blog format. Equally, this belief hindered those who wanted to blog for their business, but couldn't because of the negative public perception around blogging. And so, despite having some of the most successful tech entrepreneurs of the time, Sweden failed to achieve similar growth in the new media space.

Cheating isn't always a bad thing though. It's also a simple and effective way of creating a necessary boost to your content so that it becomes visible at all. Then, if it's good enough, your boosted visibility will turn into organic and viral visibility.

If you want to use the **cheating** tactic or principle to drive virality, you really need to combine it with one (or more) of the other principles.

Remember that in a world of organic growth, even ads are considered cheating. This in turn means that most of what you are used to doing as a company or marketer, activities that are non-organic, are also considered to be cheating if they are used to make something look more popular than it is.

It's important to note that if you want to use the **cheating** principle, your job doesn't end when you buy the vanity metrics, you also have to use them to persuade people to share your content.

The best case of this I've seen so far was when Volvo Trucks launched their "Epic Split" video to the world. We've already seen this example above in the **creativity** principle. But it's such a prime example of **cheating** too, that I had to bring it back.

The content in that video just isn't viral. Seriously, it's too damn good to go viral on its own. I will explain what I mean by that a bit later. But what's important for this part of the book is to recognize that this was *an ad for a truck steering system*.

Think about that. An ad for a truck steering system.

Now imagine calling up the Wall Street Journal and asking them to publish your truck steering system ad. What do you think their response would be?

Right... they most likely would give you a huge number that you'd have to pay to buy ad space in their publication. However, they didn't in this case. They got into the Wall Street Journal for free.

What do you think changed the minds of the thousands of publishers around the world who published stories about Volvo's truck steering system? Why didn't they charge Volvo for most of the placements in prime editorial space?

Well, as you might already have figured out. Volvo didn't call them to say they wanted to place an ad. Instead they called to say that they had the most popular piece of content online.

That flips the script.

If you have the most popular content online, publishers will be clawing down you door to get their hands on it. Their whole revenue model is built around aggregating popular content, generating traffic and earning marketing dollars. So if you are holding popular content, even if it is an ad, you won't have to buy your placement, instead you can sell it and charge for it. We briefly touched on this in the **creativity** section. Feel free to skip back and re-read that now. In the case of the *'Epic Split'* I don't think they sold their content to publishers. However, I do know that Volvo (or their representatives) used a company called BeOn to 'seed' their video in a network. And BeOn's brief was to generate 10 million views on the video.

On day one they got 3 million views, over the following two days, they had reached 6 million views in total. These were not organic views. These views were purchased.

But, of course, when Volvo started pushing out their press releases around this video, they didn't mention the fact that they had bought most of the views. Instead they wrote that "this video has received 6 million views in three days".

Once they'd heard that, publishers competed to get the Volvo content onto their platforms as quickly as possible, to try to squeeze some proximity juice (being close to popularity and getting rewarded for it) out of it.

Volvo used the **cheating** principle (knowingly or unknowingly) in order to make their content look popular. They then used this perceived popularity to get published on websites that had a lot of traffic, in order to become even more popular.

The people who saw the video on those platforms for the first time were presented with a *new* story about the story, not that Van Damme had done the epic split in 3 movies, but that *this was the most popular content online right now*. They of course felt inclined to share it with their followers on their own social media platforms. And virality took hold.

It was not the content of the video that generated the effect, but the mass hysteria around the belief that the content was popular. That's what I mean when I say that "the content in the video isn't viral." The mechanics did the trick.

This is not only evident from the many emails I received when I first wrote about this case, consisting of email correspondence between the different agencies involved in the launch. It is also publicly available by simply looking at the views graph for the video on YouTube.

A viral aggregated graph in its purest form looks like an 'S-shaped curve'. In most cases it's a little wobblier than that, as in the example below. This kind of curve is created when a piece of content is shared between users in an organic way. Most importantly it shows growth as it inclines. The shape of the curve is the pace at which it is being shared.

See viral graph here - https://goo.gl/YZX6PM

However, when the aggregated curve looks like a 'banana-gun', as in the example below, you can attribute that number of views to a manufactured launch, rather than the inherent virality of the content itself.

See cheating graph here - https://goo.gl/YZX6PM

Looking at the same graph from a daily perspective, you can see what I mean. Most the views were aggregated in the first few days of the campaign and since then only a few people have watched the video at all.

Some people question my analysis of this, pointing out that some things can "go viral" and still have a banana-shaped curve. But that is, in my mind, a misconception.

There *are* some organic cases that show a banana-shaped curve, where a video or webpage has been shared to platforms like Reddit and it receives such a huge blast of views after being upvoted by users. However, I still don't consider that to be 'viral' as it generally remains on that one platform: nobody really shares the video after that initial blast.

It is definitely 'organic', but it's not 'viral'. For a piece of content to go viral, people need to continuously share it until it reaches the limits of its natural bubble and can't be shared any more.

For a video like the *'Epic Split'*, they are competing in the entertainment bubble. The biggest viral hit in that bubble is *'Gagnam Style'*, with an insanely high view count of 2.7 billion views. That's what I mean by the "limits of its natural bubble". So, regardless of where the initial push happened, through Reddit or through spam or through ads, the *'Epic Split'* content still isn't viral. It could have gone viral as a result of the initial spam, but it didn't. As evidenced by its mere 87 million views.

It's important to make the distinction between 'viral content' and 'viral mechanics', despite the fact that *'Epic Split'* won almost all of the creative awards for viral content in the year following the ad's launch. What do the ad industry know, eh?

The mechanic they used allowed them to convince people and publishers that the video was popular. This is the fundamental success factor of the project.

Here you can see a curve that was launched using a cheating mechanism and then going viral (as you can see by the many small S-curves along the progression of the curve).

See dual graph here - https://goo.gl/YZX6PM

THROUGH CONTENT

So, I've given you a bunch of different approaches for how to **activate** people. The main theme however, and the most important thing for you to remember, is to stop communicating TO people, and start working on communicating THROUGH people.

The outdated notion that an idea or piece of content is going to move from you, as a sender, to one or more recipients, is a really inefficient way of using the internet and its billions of connections.

So you need to move towards thinking about 'through-content'. Content that is communicated *through* people rather than *to* them.

I like to break this down into three different content types. I hope to be able to develop more in the future, but these are the three major categories that I've been able to identify and repeat.

THE THREE CATEGORIES OF MESSAGING OR CONTENT ARE:
- WOW-Messaging
- ME-Messaging
- Versus-Messaging

WOW-MESSAGING

WOW-messaging is constructed from all of the theories that I've detailed above which aim to highlight a detail in a story that a user can use. The user will then use this detail to tell the world that *they know something that other people don't know yet*. In other words, this detail is a piece of a story that makes them appear special, and therefore makes a story worth sharing with other people. Because then they can be special too.

There are many applications for **WOW-messaging**. It is used a lot by brands these days and is almost always successful in generating shares.

The mindset you need to have here, is to think in terms of *what makes someone seem interesting* when they are talking about this content.

I recently read a book about how to make a great TED-talk (*'Talk Like TED'* - you can Google it and buy it on Amazon). It presents the idea that every great TED talk has three components in common. Something that generated *emotions*, something genuinely *new*, and something that people can *learn*.

For me, this fit perfectly into the idea of **WOW-messaging**. It plugs directly into that part of our brain that makes us feel good about ourselves. We feel rewarded when we experience something that makes us feel, think and grow.

So, find whatever detail you can extract and highlight in your story (remember, we call this the **story about the story**) that will make people feel, think and grow. They will find it much easier to talk about your story, photo, text or video if you do this work for them; which will in turn make them much more inclined to share.

I mean, if you don't give them something to point out about your story, the **friction** and **anxieties** associated with it will shoot up. They'll have to come up with something themselves. You need to show them a clear idea of what *the value* of reading, watching, or listening is.

WOW-messaging can be used to build everything, from the messaging on a photo, to the quotes written in backgrounds, to the headline of a YouTube video.

The perspective you need to take when labeling your content, when putting text on a photo, when writing the headline of your video, or when naming your webpage, should be: "How can this be used to communicate something about the person who is watching it, to someone else?"

I know it sounds pretty complicated. And it is difficult to grasp at first. So I've created a page on jesperastrom.com with examples to make it easier. Please ask questions either on my blog or on YouTube if you're still having problems.

I can promise you that once you *do* understand WOW-messaging, you will see a dramatic increase in the amount of shares you get of your content.

ME-MESSAGING

ME-messaging is a variation of WOW-messaging that focuses more on what the content says *about the person* who is sharing it, rather than on a specific detail in the story.

An example of **ME-messaging** is that 'share page' you get after you've completed an online psychology test. You know the ones that put you into a certain category of human? They are giving you something you can use to relate to others.

If WOW-messaging is more aligned with the **creativity** principle (remember the 5 Cs?), then ME-messaging is more tied to the **conformity** principle. Your focus should be to create content, apps and engaging material that users can use to *rid themselves of existential anxiety*. It should help them place themselves into some bigger context, to understand and establish their place in the chaotic, confusing mess that is society: "I am…", therefore I exist.

Of course this doesn't mean that ME-messaging needs to be deeply philosophical and profound. In fact cat-memes are the best example of ME-messaging out there. They help me to communicate something about myself with exactly the right tone. *Tone* is something incredibly difficult to achieve online or in text, which is why it causes existential anxiety. And that is why cat memes are so useful: because they help us to communicate.

Think about how often you text someone an "OK" as a response, only to receive an "Are you angry?" right back. We struggle to communicate even the most basic things.

Without emoji and smileys our words would be forever lost in translation, as the voice and tone of the sender is inevitably different from that of the receiver. To diffuse the kinds of misunderstandings that can arise from this, you can offer people salvation in the form of ME-messaging which they can use as a substitute for their own words.

Your focus should be to put them at the center of the content, just like we did with the Oikos project in Japan. We gave the users a simple way of saying they belonged to something, and all they had to do was hold a yoghurt next to their face and take a photo.

Hashtags are used and constructed in the same way. They help people to place their tweets and photos in a setting where other people will have an easier time of relating to them.

By enhancing your content with tools and messaging like this, you will greatly reduce the **anxiety** that people have about sharing your stuff. If you get it right, they will chose to share your content over other similar content in your particular bubble.

There are many great examples of ME-messaging out there. Like filters. With a filter, the user becomes the content, digitally filtered to be scary, funny, happy, or sad. It's a simple, visual way of users saying "this is how I feel right now, and this is who I am." The Makeup Genius app by L'Oreal is probably one of the best commercial examples of this.

MyIdol, the app where you can turn yourself into a pole dancer, was one of the first of a new breed of technologically advanced apps that help you to turn yourself into the content or story.

ME-messaging can range from simple words as text or photo-memes, to more advanced products where you build yourself into the story of a game or app. The key element of ME-messaging however, is that it enables the user to reframe the story so it's all about them. This is the ultimate example of talking THROUGH people, when they (often literally) dress themselves in your messaging and share it on their social channels.

You can see how this is fundamentally different from communicating TO someone, that they will get some specific value when they use your shit. Instead, it's a way of giving people a tool to communicate how your product has changed them.

If you are thinking like a traditional marketer, this kind of messaging will take quite a while to nail. But if you are a standard user of the web, it is probably the most intuitive of all the principles and techniques presented in this book.

VS-MESSAGING

Versus-messaging is when you give users a very simple way of selecting one of two possible outcomes. When I was working at H&M I was introduced to VS-messaging by my boss Jordan. He always used to end their Facebook posts with a closed question: "Do you want this in denim or leather?"

At first I didn't understand why we did this, but when I applied it to the conversion formula (remember, it's **Conversion** = **Motivation** + **Value proposition** + (**Incentive** - **Friction**) - **Anxiety**) it made perfect sense. By offering two alternatives I am decreasing **friction**, as the user doesn't really have to think before replying "yes" to one of them.

This is something I usually only use in debates. I set the premise for the debate by offering two opposing alternatives, which gives me a framework to control the rhetoric. When the only two options are my options, it doesn't matter which one my opponent decides to follow.

VS-messaging can be used in its simplest form by putting two alternatives next to each other and asking people to chose between them. People *love* being asked to decide between two things. You'll even find that more people will be engaged than if you were to only post one of the alternatives and ask people to suggest their own alternative. It is simply too damn difficult to think all the time. So we would rather not. Or, most of us would rather not in most situations.

Remember your 1's, 9's, and 90's? The people who don't want to think about making a choice, are your 90's. However, as we explored in the first chapter, your 1's will get in with their helpful alternatives, whilst your 9's will suggest that your limitations are wrong, and that they know what you should really be doing with your online messaging. Gotta love those 9s!

The most famous example of **VS-content** is the dress which was either blue & black or white & gold. Because of copyright issues I can't post a photo of the dress in this book (we'll get to the value of virality and Creative Commons in the next chapter when we look at **Seeding**), however if you Google "blue gold dress viral" you will find a ton of stories online covering it.

Also, whilst you're Googling things, search for "everyone wants to be a hero pepsi coke" and you'll see another great example of VS-messaging.

THE MISCONCEPTION OF GREAT CONTENT

At this point I'd like to propose some, perhaps provocative thoughts about content and quality in relation to virality. My hypothesis is that *great* content will be shared by fewer people than *useful* content.

Or in other words: if your content is too good, less people will share it, because most of them will be busy actually enjoying it.

I haven't fully investigated this idea, but the more I think and talk about it, the more and more inclined I am to believe it.

The first time it struck me was when I was at a summer festival in Sweden, doing a job for Heineken.

We had a goal of generating as much buzz around the festival activation as possible in various digital channels, to extract as much additional value as possible from it for the client. Heineken had put a lot of money into their presence at the festival and wanted to make the most of it. Our job was to make sure that happened.

During the first year of our activation we focused on building a festival area for Heineken, we jazzed it up with smoke and LEDs, and built relationships with important influencers.

The only problem was that we failed in the main activation goal. Our technology didn't work, so when people went into the little shed we had built there was actually nothing to do except for sign up to a competition on an iPad.

Many of the other sponsors had elaborate activations with wonderfully creative things to do. People were laughing and playing and partying in their activation areas. But not in ours.

For us, on the other hand, people were chilling, drinking, but not really doing what we had anticipated and hoped for. If I was to judge our results, simply by looking at the activation area, I would have deemed it a complete failure.

However, I try to never look at other people or listen to their opinions. I'd rather look at the data and study the output. And in this case, the output was astonishingly high.

Since the *only* thing people could do in our event area was to join our activation, they were being activated like nowhere else. They weren't busy playing and partying. They were busy signing up and tweeting. None of the other sponsors at the festival got as much out of their activation as us, in terms of online visibility. The closest competitor had a share of voice (in terms of shared branded content from the festival) which was five times smaller than ours, and he was one of the actual DJs playing.

These results made me really curious. So I created a test where I tried to imagine 'the world as a website', meaning that I decided to apply all of the online methods and theories that I had in my toolkit, back into the physical space of the festival activation area.

For the following year, I had prepared a series of calls to action that I used. And it worked.

Yes, we had much higher levels of activation in our activation area. Yes, people were enjoying themselves a lot more than the year before. Yes, the people from Heineken who were there to evaluate us looked happier as they left the festival.

However, when I looked at what was being shared, it was not pictures of people having fantastic and fun experiences, but instead the more mechanical elements we had put in spaces where people were surrounded with branded content.

One of these elements was a frame that we had hung from one of the sides of our activation box. On it, the frame said: "We are here, where are you?" This offered people a natural way to communicate with the digital world. Almost 50% of the people who took a branded photo, did so standing behind that frame.

When I pulled this experience through the analytical tool of the conversion formula, it made perfect sense. Everyone was **motivated** to share the fact that they were at the festival. The **value proposition** was extracted and written onto the frame ("hey, here is a simple way of boasting to your online friends who aren't here"). The **incentive** was clear, as this was the only time they could do it. The **friction** was almost zero, as they knew how to use their phones and didn't even have to write anything. And the social **anxiety** of taking a photo was completely removed, as they could always blame us if someone questioned why they took such a photo.

When we saw this we started moving our signs around so that they were in spots where people were bore. We put signs on the ground saying "selfie spot", giving people a reason to take a selfie where we knew Heineken branding would end up on the photos. We even put stickers on the backside of the toilet sink, pushing people to share as they sat down bored in the toilet.

These small changes and additions were what caused the 'internet to break' during the second year of activation. That, alongside some really neat ideas applying the same kind of formula to our collaboration with influencers, where we decreased all the **friction** associated with publishing posts by giving them VIP hospitality, photo packages, and even editing help throughout the night.

The online success we managed to generate was not due to the quality of the activation, nor was it about the excitement levels we managed to generate. It was instead the details we added that reminded people to share when they were bored, which really did the trick.

As a general rule borne out of this experience, I now always focus on designing moments of boredom into event activations. Then all it takes is to add some really powerful calls to action, and it has never gone wrong.

I have seen many brilliant activations get absolutely no shares. My conclusion is that people are so busy *experiencing* that they don't have time or see the value of sharing until it is too late. By then, their levels of **anxiety** have already increased and their dopamine levels have gone down. So, if you want to activate their share-brain again, you need to work on decreasing **friction** and providing them with compelling reasons to share that will minimize any possibility of public scrutiny.

I have also applied this logic to web apps and user funnels, only to find that they work really well there as well.

An example of this is when we created a post-purchase 'share page' on an ecommerce platform, this prompted users to share what they had purchased *after* the payment had gone through. This increased the number of shares per product by 200%, compared to the original tactic of having the share opportunity on the product page.

When you think about it, it isn't difficult to understand why this was the case. When they buy the thing they are so busy buying, comparing, asking and relating that they don't see the value of sharing. Once they are done however, they have nothing else to do but share. So they will share at a much higher rate than when they were doing the actual buying.

"Once you have the people you
need, you're one step closer
to turning your campaign
topic into a trend."

Seeding – How To Make
Sure You Reach Your Limits

Seeding – How To Make Sure You Reach Your Limits

CHAPTER 3

SEEDING TECHNIQUES

What is seeding? Seeding is about maximising the momentum that you have worked hard to build in any viral situation. It's about making sure that the *core story* isn't lost in the multitude of **smallest acceptable truths** that are being shared. It's about making sure that you get published in the places that are most relevant to your specific activation.

Seeding is a blend of old-school PR tactics and basic grunt work. In essence, you make a ton of contacts with people both inside and outside your network. You work with them until you have created a new behavior, one where people recognise your activation as *the new trend* that they should to take notice of. Once they've taken notice, they will be compelled to either share, or to express something about the thing you're promoting, in the long run, cause they have too in order to seem as though they are still on top of things.

But let's take a step back. I feel a need to properly explain what seeding is all about, as the concept has been brutally murdered by media agencies over the last few years. The mainstream belief has been that **seeding** is nothing more than simple practice of pushing your content into a network of publishers, them publishing it, and getting a lot of traffic as a result.

However, I believe that **seeding**, done well, is one of the most beautiful crafts that you can perfect in the online space. It takes years to gain mastery over truly great seeding skills.

In its essence, seeding is the art of finding *new places* where you can insert links that lead back to your content: either by getting other publishers to embed your content into their own websites; or by getting them to link to your content with basic text links.

If you get good at seeding, you'll be able to ensure that you can extract all of the potential possible value from any given initiative. For every euro you spend, you will be able to get more traffic, more revenue, more coverage, etc.

The first challenge when it comes to seeding is to find all of the places where you can seed your links. The second is to do the seeding in an organic way. And the third is to restrain yourself, and not overdo the seeding, especially if you find an automated way to seed a *lot* of links at once..

Imagine a situation where you have just run a campaign. Perhaps you created a video on YouTube, or generated a hashtag on Twitter. Perhaps you ran a TV commercial that generated a lot of buzz in blogs or on Facebook. Regardless of the format you chose, things have happened, and you're pretty pleased with yourself.

As you look at your backend data, you notice that you are only getting a fraction of all of the traffic associated with the topic of your campaign.

> *Seeding is what you need to do to get back into the discussion, helping to make sure that people are aware of your product or service when they're discussing the topic.*

> *In practice, this usually means collecting data about everyone who has been engaged and making sure that they link back to your original source in their posts or updates. You want to do this either by using your video content, your photos with references back to your website, or by ranking for the search terms that people are triggered to search for when they see your TV commercial.*

The seeding techniques I will explain in this chapter are best practices when it comes to things like:

DISCOVERY
- Notifications
- Harvesting the right keywords and hashtags
- Scraping

CONTACT OPPORTUNITIES
- Forum discussions
- Entering groups
- E-mail, and how to write a good one
- Google search, making sure you rank where people search
- Using your own network

AUTOMATION
- Syndication
- Marketing automation and notifications
- Creative Commons

DISCOVERY

In order to influence people so that they pay attention and write about you, you need to make sure that you find suitable targets. The discovery phase of seeding is full of automated and manual steps that you can go through to make sure that you find those targets. You need to find and document contact details and online locations where you can get in touch with the people you need. Once you have the people you need, you're one step closer to turning your *campaign topic* into a trend.

LOOKING AT BACKLINK REPORT

The best way of finding seeding locations is to analyze backlinks to other similar campaigns. These should be campaigns that you have run yourself, and those of competitors or other active content providers and brands in the space where you operate.

A backlink report will give you a list of publishers who have previously published and linked to the material you are querying. The tool I like to use is called majestic.com. It makes it super easy to find out who has linked to a specific url.

The classic use case for this practice is when I'm trying to get publishers to embed my YouTube videos in their publications. I simply use *Majestic* to search for all the publishers who have embedded related or similar kinds of videos, then I use the list that *Majestic* produces to guide my targeted emails or calls.

This works extremely well and makes perfect sense. If a person previously linked to a video on the same topic as your video, they are signalling that this type of content is relevant to their readers or network. They are also demonstrating that they are willing to publish this kind of content. The only thing you need to do when approaching them, is to remind them of the video they published that was similar to yours, and perhaps promise to make sure they receive a lot of traffic if they publish.

So, looking at backlink reports and exports is the first step I go through when working with any kind of seeding tactic.

HARVESTING THE RIGHT KEYWORDS AND HASHTAGS

The first thing you need to do is set up a spreadsheet with all of the keywords that might be relevant to your campaign. You should then set up trackers and notifications for these specific keywords.

There are several kinds of keywords you can target, depending on your campaign goals. However, there is a basic structure that you can follow.

EVERY KEYWORD HAS THREE COMPONENTS:
- The main thing
- A detail about the thing
- An intent about what they want to do with the thing

The more information you have on each of these three components, the more likely you are to be able take the user on a relevant journey. The more you understand what users are searching for (split into these three categories) the easier it will be to meet them with a relevant ad. And a relevant ad, will be more likely to lead to a conversion.

Consider a person searching for "shoes". If that person knows what kind of shoes they want, they will most likely add a detail like a brand or a color. Let's say they add the detail "red". The new keyword is "red shoes". It seems simplistic to say, but now we know that they're not looking for "blue shoes" or "black shoes". We still, however, don't know if they are looking to buy the red shoes or if they are just looking for more information about the category of red shoes.

But, if the keyword included an intent, then we know some more about what the user is up to. A keyword with "buy" in front of the "red shoes" would give us a much better chance of meeting the search with a relevant ad: "buy red shoes".

Funnily enough, the logic for building great ads also works when you are looking to discover who is talking about you and who would be willing to write about you. So, when using search engines like Twitter, Facebook, YouTube or Google, you should understand that you'll probably get *less hits* if you build very specific keywords that consist of the **thing**, a **detail** and an **intent**. But you probably should start there, as those expressions will be the most relevant.

The best way of extracting the right keywords is to look at what people are already saying about your activation. What are they writing when they share? What kinds of words are people using when they are making comments? What are the topics in the forums and what kind of tonality are people using when discussing your content?

The use of hashtags usually signals that a person wants to belong (remember the **conformity** principle in the previous chapter?), in which case you help them to belong, by approaching them as *someone who already belongs*. Hashtags can also signal professional usage, in which case you will find it very easy to get your message through if you can either offer some unknown facts that make the person look like more of an expert professional, or you can offer some asset that helps them to increase their social status.

WHEN SORTING THROUGH HASHTAGS YOU SHOULD THINK ABOUT:

- Your campaign name
- Whatever hashtags you previously launched
- Themed hashtags that are on topic
- Competitors' hashtags and brand names
- General related topics of interest

Once you have harvested the hashtags that you think will lead to a set of interesting people, you can move onto the next step.

NOTIFICATIONS

The next step is to set up notifications wherever possible. If you have a social media monitoring tool, this will be a quite simple process, but if you don't then this will take you a bit more time.

The best free way to set up notifications is to work with a combination of IF THIS THEN THAT (IFTTT) and (used to be) Yahoo Pipes (which sadly don't exist anymore). Using these tools you set up RSS-feeds on each of your keywords, then ask the system to notify you via your channel of choice when something changes.

If you do it right, when someone mentions you or talks about one of your defined keywords, you will be notified. Of course that will take a bit of time, so until then you can focus on working with outreach.

SCRAPING

Once you have the links, the keywords and the hashtags, you will be left with the annoying job of collecting contact information.

I like to do this with a series of different scraping methods, collecting emails and phone numbers into a database that can work from. Depending on how the source of your scrape is coded, you can set up rules so it collects and categorises information automatically from new sources as they pour in.

This is an especially effective method for social media platforms, where people often publically publish their contact details in their profiles or descriptions.

Scraping is the method of collecting contact data automatically. You can use a few programming languages to perform scraping, but if there is one I would recommend, it would be Python. There are many tools like OutWit and IFTTT that you can use to select and sort the output you get from your Python scrape. I am quite new to Python, and if you want to learn more about that programming language, I would suggest you take at least one online course before attempting to use it.

What you do with the data that you've scraped, is up to you. I have to warn you though, that scraping and data collection is highly regulated in some markets and you should take legal advice before collecting and using any kind of data.

CONTACT OPPORTUNITIES

You have to understand that every person *is a person*, driven by their own agendas and rewarded with their own currencies. In terms of the **1-9-90-model**, you already know that the **1's** are rewarded by the time and love you give them; the **9's** are rewarded by the vanity they can get out of a relationship with you, either through money or some other social or emotional currency; and **90's** are rewarded when they feel you give them something easy to consume in return for their very limited amount of input. Solve problems for your 90's and they will like you for it; give status to your 9's and they will hang around to tell your story; and give love to your 1's and they will help you achieve big things.

When working with seeding, you almost always work with your 9's. So one of your main responsibilities is to never look needy. You need to identify the *currency* of the person you are trying to influence, then make sure they know *you have it*. This will build a strong attraction between you and the person you are targeting.

This is the main construct for how you should think. Yes it is cynical, but it works, so if you want to make sure that you can extract the full value from your online activities, you should consider it.

FORUM DISCUSSION

The key concept with **seeding** is to never *push* your content to another user. Instead, always show interest in what *they* are doing and give generously to the discussion. What I have found, is that once you engage with other people online, they will naturally start researching you and whatever you represent.

This behavior creates a relationship between you and the person you have made contact with.

Over time, this relationship leads to publications of your content and links back to you, whenever they are referencing a topic that is associated with what you do. You should, in other words, set yourself up to *become a source* for people, rather than pushing your sources onto people.

This can become a very time consuming activity, so you really need to pace yourself and figure out ways to automate parts of the process. The better you get at automation the more value you'll be able to extract per hour spent on seeding.

In order for this tactic to work however, you need to prepare your platform so that it guides people back to wherever you want them to go.

This means making sure that your profile links lead to places where you will be interesting to the person you want to build a relationship with. Not only the links on your forum profile, but all of the other links on social media platforms, and on your own website.

Every person who is involved in a discussion in a forum has some kind of ego they want to protect. Either they have an ego associated with their persona, or they have an ego associated with the ideas they share. By studying what kind of sources they are sharing you will quite quickly be able to mimic their behavior. Once you do, they will feel as though you are an ally, and as a result they will start researching *you*. This doesn't work every time, but it works enough times to make it a profitable practice.

You have to use a different account for each topic you are involved in. No one wants to see that you are involved in a whole range of discussions with many different people, behaving differently or in an inconsistent manner. You need to uphold your persona in order to maintain a straight face. You need to act like a real person.

In discussions, make sure you disagree with details but agree on bigger points. This builds a sense of slight irritation in other people, which makes them look for your approval. They will feel intellectually stimulated but never scared of losing face when they are in contact with you.

Rather than posting your own links, you should try to reference the work that you have done *without linking*. This gives them the opportunity to post the link and ask for your confirmation: "Is this what you mean...?" Always go down the route of "not entirely" agreeing, as that will stir the 9's to continue their pursuit of accessing whatever it is that you have.

With practice, this becomes habit and you will be able to work on several accounts in several different tabs of your browser, without losing grip of the situation.

ENTERING CLOSED GROUPS

Groups on social platforms are different to forums. Although they look a lot alike, the culture in most groups are much more of a **conformity** situation than a **charisma** situation. If you want to be liked and referenced in closed groups, you have to adapt to the general philosophy of the group you are working in.

I don't know why this is the case, but my best guess is that people turn to closed groups to feel safe from the kind of scrutiny they can face in the public world. Perhaps groups are more nerdy and maybe that leads to a more 1-driven culture, but to be honest, I have no clue. I just know that if I work from a **conformity** angle, closed group work becomes much easier than if I try to run with the **charisma** tactic that I generally use in open forums.

The general tactic to establish yourself in a closed group is *reciprocity*. You should work on understanding who the most active users are and how much they weigh-in on a discussion. You should identify their blogs, YouTube accounts and other similar resources.

The second step is to use content that they have produced historically, the older the better, to make updates in the group or as comments on other people's posts. Not only will this behavior lead to people using *your* content as responses, but it will also lead to people *pinging* you, asking for your input in discussions where you are not active. This is especially likely if they think you might pick something to reference that they have produced in the past.

So, when working with seeding in groups, you need to understand the group culture and the group influence structure, then exploit both to the point where you come out as knowledgeable enough to be referenced by people.

Perhaps it's a bit sad, but it's also interesting to see how blind and biased people become when they feel that you are a part of their team. As long as you use the group's terminology - which you'll learn quite fast - you will have the *benefit of the doubt* in almost anything that you do. If you post a controversial video, the group will interpret it from the most generous and positive perspective they can. If you share a blog post where you have linked to them, they will generally share it to express your awesomeness. If you are attacked by an outsider, they will rally to support you.

This is the most efficient way I have found of working in groups. Stay humble, stay cynical and share other people's sources. Sooner than you think, they will start mimicking your behavior.

E-MAILS AND HOW TO MAKE THEM COUNT

For a few years now, I have read that less and less people read and send email. This has led to a huge misconception in the marketing world that outreach via email is something highly ineffective.

However, looking at the average conversion rates from email published by the big ecommerce players, I know that we still have many many years to go before we can remove *sending emails* from our toolbox of seeding techniques.

The following section is mostly focused on writing emails to people you *don't* have an established relationship with, however, it should work splendidly in any situation where you use email as your communication medium of choice.

Regardless of how you have gathered the email send list, the general rule is to personalize your emails as much as possible. Depending on the type of user you are emailing (meaning a **1, 9 or 90**) you need to format your introduction accordingly.

There are many tools you can use to find out someone's personality. The best I am using right now is called *'Crystal Knows'*. They have a plugin for Gmail, and as long as they can find the person associated with the email address in their databank, they can suggest a templated version of an email for you, based on the specific purpose you have for writing that email.

In most cases, I use some form of automation when emailing, especially if I have scraped big lists of email addresses. However, when I'm trying to reach out to journalists and big bloggers, I have found that spending a bit more manual time on every email makes it worthwhile in the end.

As long as I have the right tools to support with basic profiling and to gain an understanding of what formats these journalists like to publish in, I generally have no trouble in getting a response from them. The real craftsmanship comes in writing a good subject line for the email. Once you get an *open*, you can work over time to get a *click* and then a *reply*.

For panic campaigns, ie. where you have very little time to execute them, and you have no prior relationship, you will have to increase the amount of automation you use, as well as the volume of the network you are trying to seed to. You will have to go for people with a high degree of *topic relevance*, as you simply have prior relationship, and there's no way that they will have mentioned your campaign previously.

Every email follows the same structure though.

Start each one with the **value proposition** for what they'll get if they read the rest of the email. This means you need to look carefully at whatever *currency* the receiver might feel rewarded by, and establishing a reference to that first.

If I am writing to a lifestyle blogger, I would probably start with something in the vicinity of: "I saw your photos from [insert club name], and would like to extend an invitation to something on another level". If I was writing to a journalist, I would probably go with a: "I read your very well read article about [insert topic], and would like to hand you some information that could possibly be the basis for a follow-up".

The second thing you should do is to place yourself into an attractive context. This means making sure that you humbly mention that you are a superstar within the area you are trying to represent.

The third thing is to provide a link to a place where the receiver can read the full story or download the resources they need to publish something about you.

The fourth is to write out a short outline, preferably a bullet list, of what they can find out if they press the link. This should encourage them to want to click the link you have just given them access to.

The fifth is to create *two ways* in which the receiver can move forward. Both of which are positive, and both of which mean a *yes* for you. In the world of vacuum cleaner sales, this would be the equivalent of offering the customer to pay right now, or in 30 days. Or, putting this in terms of **VS-messaging**, you should focus on giving them a closed question where they select between your two favorable options, rather than the option of doing one thing, or nothing at all.

The final thing you should write, is what will happen if the receiver doesn't comply with the two options you have given them above.

I understand that this seems like a very long email, but you will have to balance good content with length: it is a tradeoff. Remember the rules of the **conversion formula**. For every line of copy you write, the more **friction** you add for completing the e-mail. So you have to practice a lot and edit a lot in order to make the perfect email.

GOOGLE SEARCH

Now listen. If there is one thing that is seriously underused when brands are trying to contact people who are looking for specific keywords associated with their activation. It is that they are often not really present in Google search.

I have seen this SO MANY TIMES. Brands spend millions on activating people through TV-commercials, Facebook campaigns, banner ads etc, for keywords and campaign names that have no real representation in Google searches.

This is the dumbest waste of money in the world.

The way to be present in Google searches is to either create content pages on your website that are in line with Google best practices, and therefore rank organically. Or, to buy AdWords for the keywords that people start searching for when you run your campaigns.

Most of the time, a combination of the two is the best practice that I recommend. Often you'll need some time to rank for the keywords that you want, so until you rank organically, you should definitely buy these search results with Google ads.

There is a classic example from the Swedish market where an electronics chain ran an ad on TV where they used an old rapper to say the words "bike when you buy, bike when you buy" about a hundred times within 30 seconds.

The result of this repetitive activation was that tons of people started searching for "bike when you buy" on Google ("bike when you buy" translates to "cykel på köpet" in Swedish. Check it out in Google Trends. Choose Sweden, select the years '2004 until today'. It is funny.)

> It was a weak form of a **story about the story**, applying the **creativity** principle. However, since their media budget was obviously huge, the repetition of the phrase was enormous. People bought into it and started looking them up on the offer.

> The only problem was that the electronics company didn't have a single link in Google that met the demand of the searchers. Instead, a user called "MrBaddare" had downloaded the ad and published it on his/her YouTube account, without any links back to the relevant store.

> Since the YouTube video was the most relevant content on the internet for these thousands of searches, MrBaddare got all of the secondary value and all the commercial searches associated with the campaign.

> I can only begin to wonder how much money they needlessly lost by not understanding this mechanic. It would have been so easy to fix!

Being available in Google, being present, and being visible, is what I consider to be a baseline. It's the most basic thing you need to do as a brand. Yet most brands still don't even seem to care about it.

If you want to create a ripple effect. If you want people to be able to use the right resources, build backlinks to you, or simply to be able to contact you to show their engagement or ask questions for interviews. Then you have to be present in Google for the keywords that people start searching for, when you run your activation.

If you're not present in Google, then other people at best, or your competition at worst, will take the opportunity to earn all of the secondary value you're creating by running your activation. There simply aren't enough people in any network you can gather, who can match the amount of people tapping away on search engines.

USING YOUR NETWORK FOR SEEDING

If you have an established network, and you know who your 1's, your 9's and your 90's are, you should try to activate them through seeding efforts.

The best way to do this is to collect all the sources that you think you need people to interact with. Then you simply give the people in your network different assignments, depending on their behavioral type. For a 1, I would ask for content like guest blog posts or statistical research that can be rewritten and pitched to publishers or bigger 9's in your own network. Perhaps you already have the necessary relationships in your own network to be able to build a sufficient platform or share of voice online, to give your activation its own life.

In the Oikos case that I mentioned in the previous chapter, we had to work with seeding and connecting different users, 9's and fans, with each other, until we had a critical mass of content published online for it to seem like a trend. The *trend* then led to other influencers picking it up. Once that happened, our involvement didn't have to be as dominant anymore and we could focus on making sure everyone had the necessary resources to continue talking about us.

When we worked with Kung Fury, we used our network to help us spread the word on Reddit, and to contact local journalists. We couldn't speak many of the languages where we wanted to be published, so local backers of the project - both 9's and 1's - helped in translating and contacting the right local people. We even interviewed some of our local backers to find local **stories about the story** that would make sense in different local markets. All of the interviewees we found in our own network.

When I worked with Pepsi, we used our network to gather photos and videos from hundreds of different sales locations. This enabled us to post at a higher frequency than we otherwise would have been able to, as well as use relevant content for local pushes when we contacted press and store owners around Sweden.

AUTOMATION

Automation has become such a vital part of my everyday job in the past few years. There are several types of automation. Some which are associated with push, and some which are more inbound (pull) tactical approaches.

SYNDICATION

The most common form of automation is sharing **syndication** with other websites. This basically means that you promise to publish links to their content, and in turn, they publish links to yours. Since you have an agreement and mutual trust, you manifest this collaboration on your own platform through the introduction of related articles, widgets and feeds. If you do it right, you won't even have to publish any new content manually. Instead, it should update itself.

There are a few syndication services out there depending on whether you are publishing video, images, apps, or webpages. I keep an updated list on my website jesperastrom.com which you can check out. But as always, don't use if you don't share. If you find something new out there on the web, you should bring it to the rest of our attention.

Syndication essentially gives you an automated way of pushing links to your content out to other websites.

MARKETING AUTOMATION AND NOTIFICATIONS

Marketing automation is an expression which is predominantly used as B2B. It is a fancy way of talking about inbound marketing and lead qualification. And those things in turn are just fancy words for *sending relevant emails automatically* whilst convincing a user to buy something expensive.

However, smart marketing automation techniques can be used in many ways. One of the ways I find them truly helpful is when I try to find out which visitors to my websites are big influencers, or when I'm trying to get an unknown visitor to one of my social accounts to send me their email address.

Currently I use an excellent emailing system - *drip.co* - which gives me the ability to setup user funnels for different contacts, sending them an automated set of emails. Depending on how they react to certain emails, the next one they receive will be adjusted.

The most value I have gained when using these kind of systems is from working with huge seeding lists. Meaning, when I have scraped a lot of contact details and want to email them all individually. If I had to do this manually I simply wouldn't be able to keep track of who opened, and when, and why. No, instead I only want to put my focus on those who respond to me. All the hard work around getting opens and clicks in the initial emails, I want to set that up so it is done as automatically as possible.

So, I set up one chain of emails for users who *do not open* the emails. And once they *do* open the emails, I get them to follow a new chain of emails until they click any *link* in an email. Depending on what link they click and what they do next, that will determine what kind of communication I will send their way in the future: what new chain they go down next.

This system helps me grade different users based on their activities. I know that users who have visited the *press or media section* of my website are more likely to be publishers, so I want to take care of them first. Hence, I assign a value to those pages which is higher than other pages, and the marketing automation system helps me to track the amount of points that associated with specific email addresses.

Again, this saves me a lot of time and helps me to prioritize.

CREATIVE COMMONS

The last, but really the first thing you should do, is to make your photos and videos available on Creative Commons. There is absolutely no reason whatsoever to keep any other license on your material if you want it to be shared online.

Your content is still protected, but it is now available for remixes and alternations, making it *a lot more interesting* for people who are working with content and online publication.

Simultaneously, you solve a problem of people using poor quality material from your campaign or brand (which they will anyway), as they can now download and use whatever resources you make available. Important to note is that adding Creative Commons, with attribution as a requirement, takes care of much of the otherwise painstaking work of getting backlinks to your website.

It won't solve everything, but it builds a base for everyone who's looking to use your content, decreasing the friction between the thought of using it, and actual production. This naturally increase the inclination by the publisher to use your content in their own posts.

"you want it to blow up and become something that a lot of people understand and get involved with."

Bubble Transition – How To Make Sure You Break Your Limits

Bubble Transition How To Make Sure You Break Your Limits

CHAPTER 4

BUBBLE TRANSITION & TARGETING

All the big platforms on the web have so much content that it's literally impossible for them to show you everything that's available every time you use them. So to counter this problem, they have developed indexes that show you whatever *they think you might find most relevant* at any point in time.

The selection processes they use are based on a series of variables which are processed through an algorithm. Although there are many cases where human quality checks still occur, most of the time the content that shows up in front of you has been placed there automatically, and is based on who you are, where you are, and how you have behaved in the past.

THERE ARE A 5 VARIABLES THAT SEEM TO GOVERN MOST OF THE PLATFORMS:

Topicality: the topics you have an interest in
Sentiment: your preferences in relation to those topics
Relationship: your personal relationship with the content or its sender
Locality: where in the world you currently are and where you *usually* are
Device: the kind of device (tablet, smartphone, PC) you are viewing the content from

All of these variables play a significant role when the algorithm tries to determine what content is going to be shown to you.

At the same time as it is trying to figure out what you want to see, it is also trying to figure out what you *don't* want to see. People have referred to the result of this process as a "filter bubble", where you only end up seeing the kind of stuff that *you like to see.*

Contrary to popular understanding, that doesn't mean you won't see things you don't agree with. But it does mean you *will* only see things that engage you, that please you, and that make you feel satisfied.

Sadly, as marketers this makes our lives difficult. It means that even the ads we run are more likely to be shown to people who *already like* the stuff that is in the ads. This means that a lot of people we want to reach just won't be shown the content that we want them to see.

This is probably the biggest argument against traditional paid advertising, as it will generally only be useful to confirm people who already like your thing, rather than to help you build your audience.

In order to build an audience you need to use *people* (as always). This is where the value of understanding the **1-9-90** relationship plays a big role.

Every topic, place, and relationship has its own set of 1's, 9's and 90's. When we think about them as an aggregate group, they are *the group* of people who are able to see content about that specific topic, place or relationship when they are logged into one of the big platforms (Twitter, Facebook, Snapchat, etc.)

Consider *yourself.* You are interested in some topics (a 90), quite expressive about others (a 9), and absolutely nerdy about very few (a 1). You don't have the time or mental space to know something about everything in the world, but you can know something about many things. Your knowledge varies to different degrees, based on how close you are to a topic, person, or place that is mentioned online.

The index algorithms of Google, Facebook, Instagram and many others are trying to mimic this real world situation in a digital setting. Why? Well ultimately so that you feel comfortable using their services, and you keep coming back.

But, luckily for us marketers, these indexed platforms aren't the only thing out there. For example, most blogs and newspapers aren't indexed, meaning that they show the *latest* or *most popular* story of the day on their front page. Everyone who enters their websites gets the same story, regardless of prior behavior.

The same thing goes for your messaging app of choice and your SMS service. It is not the most *popular* discussion you have had with your friends that pops up at top of the app when you log in. No, instead it is the latest message you sent.

From a different perspective we can also view platforms like Reddit as a type of non-indexed platform that will become increasingly important for you. Although Reddit is a curated platform, where you see the most upvoted links, it still displays the same results for everyone. This means that there is an added layer of irrelevance to you at times, but it also means you get to see stories you would have otherwise not seen.

As a marketer these types of platforms become *essential* to launch content through, as this is the kind of place where users get the resources and the content that they end up sharing on Facebook.

CONSIDER THIS SCENARIO:
A 1 creates a blog post about the underlying causes of cancer and exemplifies this with a tale about Djingis Kahn. The 1 publishes the blog post on a domain that she owns and posts it to Facebook. This topic will now only be seen by people who are likely to either be interested in cancer causes, Djingis Kahn, or who have a prior relationship with the 1 who created the story.

In order to make the story go further than the three bubbles above, we have to either make it topically relevant or relationally relevant to someone else.

This work is done by the 9's who pick up the story and make it accessible to others, through their commentary and remixes of the story. Perhaps they draw it up as a cartoon, they might list a series of celebrities who might have personal experiences from that story, or they create a video with clips from doctors that turn the article into a rap.

Whatever means they use to make the information accessible is up to them. However, they have turned it into something that can exist in a bigger bubble than the initial content. In this bigger bubble there are other 9's, who will make their own interpretations etc, and so the content goes viral.

Now imagine *you* want to get something out there.

If you have a network (which you should have by now, if you've been following along with this book), then you will be able to reach out to your 1's and ask them to publish content about the topic you want to get out into the world. Perhaps you write an initial blog post or publish a video that you want them to build upon.

Whatever they do can be considered as prototypes for content that might contain details for your 9's. Who will then be able to translate that narrow content into something consumable by a broader audience.

Now, once you have a few pieces of content produced by your network, you need to seed that content so that your 9's see it. As your initial networked 9's respond and do their remixes, you will experience some growth and attract some traffic. However, eventually that traffic will start to diminish as the amount of people who are connected to them, runs out. You've reached the limit of your bubbles.

But, you have bigger ambitions for your story, as you want it to blow up and become something that a lot of people understand and get involved with.

This is when you start focusing on what I like to call **bubble transition**. This is the idea that you can use the prototypes of content from your 1's, and the newly created stories from your networked 9's, together with some advertising, in order to reach new 9's and 1's who will be able to give their perspective on the topic and introduce it into new bubbles.

TREND AND MECHANIC PAIRING

The most common tactic for doing this is **trend and mechanic pairing**. In this tactic you look for online trends and try to inject your concept into them, using the **Creativity** principle.

THE "ICE BUCKET CHALLENGE" IS A PERFECT CASE STUDY FOR THIS TACTIC.

Initially, the same mechanic was used in a German beer challenge where users were asked to down a pint of beer in one minute, then challenge three of their friends to do so within 24 hours. If the friends didn't respond, they had to buy the challenger a full case of beer.

This challenge was hugely successful and spread all over Germany and some other European countries.

Someone from the "Ice bucket challenge" team must have seen the trend and understood that there was an underlying mechanic that could be duplicated and placed in another creative setting.

So, they took the central concept of 'one challenger and 3 challenged'. They also took the challenge mechanic where the challenged had to respond within 24 hours. They added the ALS message on top and used the Charisma principle to launch the activity through some celebrities, which kickstarted the challenge in some really big bubbles.

Since the challenge existed on both indexed and non-indexed platforms, it was able to grow unhindered by people's pre-existing profiles, and it moved from challenger to challenged without a problem.

Or, perhaps put in other words, since the challenge was one where you tagged people, they got notified via e-mail and notification. This "hacked" the index algorithms, as people got notified regardless of how relevant Facebook thought the content was for them.

As more people joined, the challenge was introduced into more bubbles. Not only through the number of challenges being produced, but also because of the number of publications covering the progress of the challenge. Everything from bloggers to journalists teamed up to write their story about the story. Some focused on the ALS-issue, whilst others focused on the craziness of the challenge itself. All of which increased the Motivation for people to join, and decreased the Anxiety of pouring cold water over one's head.

Now, consider this from a **bubble transition** perspective. They took an existing trend & mechanic that was being shared between bubbles. Copied it and put it into their own context. Then used people who were celebrities who would connect them to big bubbles based on their relationship with their fans, in order to launch the challenge.

The mechanic then took care of the jump between different bubbles as it moved between big and indexed platforms like as YouTube and Facebook, into blogs and email where new users could discover it and share it into their own bubbles.

The most common tactic to transcend between bubbles has been to study online trends and copy whatever prototype takes off. Copy the mechanics, and put it into your own context. Then, if you don't have access to celebrities, launch it to the people who were engaged in the previous trend.

Now consider this. Publishers are really keen on finding follow ups to popular stories. So you should always seed your copycat mechanic to journalists who have covered the previous story, as they will be more than willing to write the follow up story: "Is this the next ice bucket challenge?"

By taking your creative concept and pairing it with current trends and mechanics, you make it accessible to more bubbles and will be able to make a transition from your original network to new networks.

CUSTOM AUDIENCES TARGETING INFLUENCERS BEFORE CONTACT

Now, there are ways you can beat the system *even more*. One of these ways is to use **influencer targeting in custom audiences**. This is a form of nudging where you prepare the people you are about to contact, with the kind of information you want to pitch to them, before you actually officially make first contact.

The best way to do this is to target influencers with ads you know will reach them.

Imagine you want to reach the team at the Wall Street Journal. Some of them have their email address in their Twitter profiles. What you could do is to collect their email addresses and contact them directly. However, they must get a thousands of people doing this every day.

A better approach would be to reach them in an environment where they aren't as overloaded with people trying to connect with them. Two such places are Google and Facebook, where you are allowed to target people using their email address, if they are already a *customer* of yours.

Since these people aren't your customers or a part of your network, you have two options. Either you bait them until they sign up to something that you can offer, or you don't give a crap about Facebook and Google's rules and just target them anyways.

My internal ethical discussion has concluded that I should do my very best to reach out to them and get them to opt-in, but that I also have a right to target them, given that they have written "contact me here" next to their email address.

Now I know this is controversial, and you will have to make up your own mind about what you want to do. The only thing I suggest you HAVE to do is to check with someone who knows your domestic legislation before proceeding. In some countries, the use of personal data for targeting, might be considered illegal, regardless of where you collected the data.

If you decide to proceed with creating custom audiences from the emails you collected, you should do so with the understanding that you'll have to *tweak your messaging to fit the recipients*. Because of the algorithmic priorities of Google and Facebook you will have to make sure that the content is topically relevant for the receiver in order to show up in their feed. This is essential regardless of whether or not you are paying for it as an ad.

So, use the **Creativity** principle and the **conversion formula** to tweak your story so it fits the frame of mind of the receiver. Or in the jargon of this book: pretend to *be your own 9*.

Your network might want to help you out with this task, but ultimately you have to be the decision maker of what goes live as the ads test on the platform.

If you do decide NOT to use the emails, you can use each platform's own targeting tools to reach very niche groups of people. Do not use their targeting based on *interest*, but rather use targeting that focuses on *"works in"*, along with demographic data and income data. That will be much more likely to hit the right target.

For the platforms that allow you to use keyword targeting, I would recommend you to run a text analysis on whatever the person has written - as this is probably what the platform algorithm has used - in order to find relevancy and build a profile for the kind of person you are trying to reach. (I have listed a few tools to run an analysis like this on jesperastrom.com). Then simply add those keywords to your targeting in order to filter out irrelevant people.

If you decide not to use the emails, the targeting will take a lot more time, but it will be equally as effective if you decide to use keyword targeting.

Once you're done with the **targeting** you can move onto the **messaging**. It should come as no surprise that I think you need to test several different **stories about the story** until you find one that you get a lot of interactions on. *That* is the messaging you should now use for your email subject and content of your email to your influencer.

If you want to go back to the **seeding** chapter and look at how to write a good email, then now is a good time to do so.

The psychology and power of preparing a recipient by using targeted ads, is really astonishing. When I run these kinds of campaigns I generally increase my open rate from close to 0% up to 50-60%. Of course this requires training, patience, and determination. But if you start using it, you will see how you can quickly become increasingly good at both the *targeting* and *messaging* over time. And your hit results will increase.

I suppose the success of this has a lot to do with a sense of urgency (**incentive** in the conversion formula). The publisher who sees my ads might not click them, but the topic builds in importance inside their brain, and that might be why they are more willing to open my emails.

I always set my campaigns to have a *frequency per user* which is set to seven plus. This means that an ad will show at least seven times to a user before it stops showing. For me, this means that the user has almost definitely seen the content and is more likely to open the email from me later.

In some instances, the ad alone has been enough for me to get an email *directly* from the publisher wanting to know more. So you shouldn't completely discount these types of campaigns as a *cost of performance*, but always try to close the contact as soon as possible in the process.

WORKING INSIDE AND OUTSIDE YOUR BUBBLE

Many brands are really good at posting *confirming* content into their own bubble. They are really good at advertising their own content to reach the limits of their bubble. However, they aren't very good at working consistently to build stories that travel between platforms and across bubbles.

This is a shame, as a lot of online content is discovered on one platform and then shared onto another.

I usually say that *"the best tactic for Facebook growth, is not being on Facebook"*. People like to share things they do outside of Facebook, on Facebook. So I develop the kinds of tactics I explained in the Heineken case study, where I try to connect physical environments with digital ones, by understanding how to convert a user to a specific behavior.

I then try to create a story on the platform where the user lands, that follows up on the previous action. Sometimes I like to refer to this as **sequential marketing**. You need to understand that each user journey has a starting point. You then need to be able to follow the user from that starting point where you have activated her, onto whatever next steps she might take. You need to change your story so that it fits in sequence with the previous piece of story you've created.

One great example of this kind of thinking is to reach users through advertising and ask them to Google something. You can then either rank organically for that keyword, or buy an ad that will show up to the user who is searching. They will follow the link from Google and land on a landing page where you ask them to share something to a *third platform* in order to unlock some secret.

Once they've unlocked the secret, they will be prompted NOT to reveal it to their friends, inducing them to want to tell their friends even more, and so the circle is closed, and you have successfully transitioned out of your bubble.

By moving users between multiple platforms, you'll be able to move them inside and outside of the indexed algorithms, making whatever they do, relevant in more bubbles. A side benefit to this is that you're able to set more cookies on each person, enabling you to retarget them on several different platforms and building an even more compelling story based on previous actions taken.

This also gives you the opportunity to target them cross-platforms, and sometimes even cross-device.

In the context of moving inside and outside the index, you also need to understand that it is sometimes better to write a blog post and advertise it on Google or send it via email to your current network, and ask them to share it on Facebook; than it is to publish the link directly on Facebook and advertise it to your network there.

The effect of that content being introduced into more "filter bubbles" by your network, with the accompanying **story about the story** (the text a user writes to explain why they shared) is many times more likely to get reach, than simply giving users the opportunity to directly react on your Facebook post.

If they didn't discover your content on Facebook, users will feel an obligation to bring it into the platform. But, if they discovered it already on Facebook, they might feel like it is already there, and so the **value proposition** and **motivation** for sharing it will decrease.

That is why it's important to move inside and outside of the big indexed platforms to get the most out of your communication; as you are able to transition between different bubbles limited by topicality, relationship or sentiment.

DIRECTING THE HATE/LOVE OF YOUR SUPPORTERS OUTSIDE YOUR BUBBLE

To build on the tactic above, it is an interesting tactic to move your lovers, meaning your 1's and 9's, from inside your small bubble, out to well trafficked non-indexed platforms. Especially if something negative has been posted about you on the non-indexed platform.

Ok. To put that into other words that make more sense.
Imagine someone has written a really bad article about you that is factually inaccurate. You have some facts disproving the hypothesis the angry writer has tried to build. This gives you a perfect opportunity to send your supporters to the article to defend your position.

The way to do this is by posting a link to the negative article on a platform where you are indexed to *only reach the people who find you relevant*. Somewhere like Facebook or YouTube. You then give your supporters the *three best arguments* against the published article.

This tactic arms your supporters with things that they can use in the comments field of the negative article. This is good for two reasons:

They have something to say that opposes the author of the negative article, which will increase both **anxiety** and **friction** for the author to do follow up stories (if they are not completely insane)
It shows readers of the negative article that there is another side to the story. All the people who now come to the article read its point of view, but when they read the comment section they will see that 40 people have strongly objected, and so their trust in the article will rapidly diminish

This is a great way of building PR online and working with negative publications. But very few brands dare to try it. They think it might create negative blowbacks on them if they try to engage their fans in these types of activities. Both in terms of bringing negative stories to their fans, but also by accidentally enraging a journalist.

What they don't get, is that the *calling* on Facebook or YouTube to engage with the negative article simply won't show to people who it isn't relevant for. It will only show to the *most engaged people* on that issue. They will be using the platform's algorithms to their favour.

Secondly, most brands don't see the value of having commentators on a non-indexed platform to drive the brand's perspective for them. They want to do everything themselves. With that philosophy however, it is very difficult to generate any kind of scalable growth in a networked world. Going viral becomes a matter of chance, rather than a matter of hard work and smart tactics.

But, if you're one of those brands, there are some "chicken alternatives". You can create user groups for the specific purpose of working with seeding and responding. You can send emails to your customers who have showed a 1-behavior and a 9-behavior, or you can simply create a messaging group with your 10-20 most engaged fans.

Either way you will be able to mobilize your supporters.

The downside of doing these kind of things in the dark, is that you risk getting caught doing it. What you are willing to do in the open, it will never become a story that your enemies can spin in a way that it affects your relationship with your hardcore fans. However, if you do stuff in the dark, journalists love to tear you apart using *trust arguments*. This might seriously damage your relationship, conversion rates, and engagement amongst your core users and network.

RETARGETING USING COOKIES AND PIXELS

Both Google and Facebook are offering you to embed a **pixel** on your website. This enables you to **retarget** users who have visited the site. This is an extremely good way of reminding people that *they have done something valuable* by visiting you.

So, why would it be important to remind people they have spent their time valuably?

Well, most people feel that they have too little time for themselves. Most of the time, brands and other people are *asking* for their time. Very few brands, or friends for that matter, contact people just to say how amazing they think they are. Usually, there is an undertone of something else in the things we communicate.

This is an opportunity that brands shouldn't miss out on. Just being open and appreciative, with no other agenda.

Equally, when more people start adopting the more celebratory retargeting approach, it will most likely continue to work, as people will always enjoy being told that they have made a good decision.

So, you might ask what value does this bring to you? Well, what I have found, is that people are very happy to share their good decisions. So if I want to break into a new bubble, I can offer people the opportunity to share that decision by using **through content.**

A lot of people are shy about bragging. What you can offer them is a way of bragging where they can blame you if it backfires. At the same time, you will be reconfirming the purchase and their positive behavior, making them feel that the relationship they are creating with you is increasing in value, as their belief in their decision has grown in importance.

Time for an actual example I think. How about two? One which is based on sharing content, reminding the user that they were one of the first to share; and another that shows how to use this in ecommerce to help your products go viral.

EXAMPLE 1: ATTRACTING ATTENTION TO A CAMPAIGN

Imagine you have posted a video to YouTube or Facebook. A user has engaged with the video early on and perhaps shared it. What they have done is not that important actually. What's important is that they have done something they remember.

When you decide to retarget people, you probably shouldn't retarget people who have seen less than 50% of the video content as they are less likely to remember that they saw the video to begin with.

Your video has gathered enough views for it to sound like a lot. Perhaps 100,000 views in two days.

Now is the perfect time to remind the user that they were ahead of the curve. They watched the video before everyone else jumped on the bandwagon. You do this by creating an ad that you deliver to that person, where you sit in front of the camera, holding a computer with the video rolling in the background, talking to the viewer with an intimate and personal tone of voice.

"Hey, I'd just like to thank you for being one of the first people who joined us by watching this video. Oh, how do I know? Well, YouTube and Facebook allows me to retarget those who saw more than 50% of the first video. That means I still don't know who you are, and so this is the only way I can thank you! If you want to let me know who you are and give me the chance to properly thank you, you can contact me on xxxxx@xxxx.com"

The above is just an example of how a video like this could turn out. You explicitly use the fact that you can retarget people who have seen the video. You can thank them and deliver a big vanity metric that makes them feel as though they have been part of something huge. This makes them likely to share this with their friends, either directly or by posting the initial video again.

Secondly, you use the fact that YouTube and Facebook doesn't give you their specific user details, to your own advantage. You come across as transparent, and it is therefore highly likely that the person watching will feel motivated to contact you to receive a proper 'thank you'. That way, you will grow your network, and the person might even post something else about your campaign or project.

EXAMPLE 2: GETTING MORE SALES OF A PRODUCT
The second way you can use this type of targeting is when a user has just bought a product.

Most brands stop retargeting users once they have completed a purchase. If they do continue to communicate with the user, it's more than likely because they have forgotten to place a burn cookie that stops the user from being retargeted by the product they have just bought.

I believe both practices are big mistakes when you consider the fact that people are happiest about their purchase at the time of purchase and for a few days after the purchase. Even before they have actually received the product or full experience.

There has been research in the travel industry, where they found that people experience the most amount of joy in the period of time between buying tickets and actually travelling. This definitely holds true for other niches. There is a vast difference in shares from people shortly after they've purchased, compared to when they have received the product. We also know that people are more likely to buy stuff that their friends have recommended to them. Hence the reason for setting up a sharing mechanic that takes care of users, reconfirming their purchase after they have placed it, in order to try and get them to share their purchase story with others. This has both a financial as well as a behavioral benefit.

*The first pitch for them to share should come on the "thank you page" of the purchase. You should focus it on something like: "you have one chance to tell your friends about the deal you just made", rather than focusing on "share your purchase with your friends". Remember from the conversion formula that you should focus on what a person gets (**value proposition** and **incentive**) in your conversion copy, rather than what they have to do to get it.*

The second pitch for them to share should be put in a story on Facebook or YouTube. You should place a test result *in their feed where the product that they bought comes out on top. The test can be performed by yourself or by a third party, but the important thing is that the product they bought should be in the top 3 of a top 10 list. That way they feel proud that they made that purchase and will probably want to share the story with their friends.*

To produce that pitch, simply write up a blog post where you put the product in a toplist. If you want to run several promotions at once, make the post accessible only through the ad. You'll see a lot of traffic from this activity, as well as a lot of shares and often a lot of purchases.

The best practice here is also to target any new visitors with a coupon code or freebee. You should reward them with this only when they give away their email address on your landing page.

All in all, these two ways you can use retargeting to increase the organic growth of your campaign or ecommerce page, will help you to stop pushing content to the already-engaged consumers inside your own bubble, and start supporting your existing customers to tell positive stories about their own purchases in *their own bubbles*. Remember, it's much more powerful to speak **through** people than to them.

This will not only increase your overall traffic, but also help you boost your **conversion** rate, as the new traffic that comes from the network/user shares, is more likely to convert into buyers than any of the traffic you get from any other source (except for perhaps your email traffic).

48 HOUR LAUNCH TACTIC

I suppose this is as good a time as any to bring up my **48 hour launch tactic**. It's the method I use to wrap all of the tactics above into one, to burst out of filter bubbles and incentivise more 9's to join in.

Ok. I should do less boasting, and more telling. Let's get to it!

The **48 hour launch tactic** is a sequential marketing tactic where you use your network to help build your story and make it grow over the duration of 48 hours. The main idea here is that you use your media budget, or your network, to reward anyone who participates by publishing your stuff.

Most brands spend their money on buying traffic to their own sources. However, as we can clearly see from most of the case studies we looked at so far, third party mentions pull in way more high quality traffic than our own adverts possibly ever could. The conversion rates are higher from that traffic, the time spent on site is higher, the number of pages visited is higher, and the length of video consumed is higher.

So, the best tactic to boost your own content is actually by promoting *content about your content*: this inevitably delivers great referrals.

There are many ways to do this, but I like to look through Google Analytics (or similar tools) for different referrals to my site, and how the traffic from different sources behaves on my website or when engaging with my content.

I try to discover the source or referral that delivers the best kind of traffic. This means that I generally go to the *referral* tab of the analytics tool I'm using and look for referrals that have resulted in a lot of shares, purchases, downloads or whatever I have set as the goal for that specific landing page.

Then I go to my ads system and create a *lookalike audience* for that page. A lookalike audience can be created in both Google and Facebook, if you have installed their cookies properly. I generally use Facebook more than Google for this. I then target the lookalike audience with the article or referral that has been delivering good traffic back to me.

The logic behind doing this, is that *that referral*, for some reason, has the ability to prepare visitors to do what I want them to do once they reach my page. So, I'd rather "wash them" through this referral instead of sending them directly to my landing page. To sort the promising leads from the unpromising ones.

So, that is the base tactic.

When applied to the **48 hour launch tactic** you put the same kind of mechanic into a sequential order where you use the referrals you get - meaning the first people who mention your content - as your advertising material to push to lookalikes of those people who visited your page from that original piece of content.

Step one is to create the content that you want to share.

Step two is to contact your 1's and ask them to co-create their own versions of the content.

Step three is to advertise your 1's stories towards the 9's you have identified until you hit a frequency of seven on your ad.

Step four is to reach out to those 9's with the content you created and pitch them to comment on the story. Sometimes you'll have to prepare their comment for them in a 'press kit' or by giving them some kind of exclusive access.

Step five is to take whatever publication you've got from the 9's and get them a load of cheap and crappy traffic that will give them as high **vanity metrics** as possible. Just buy the living crap out of the cheapest traffic around. The 9's will see the spike in their statistics dashboards (yes, all 9's follow statistics ferociously) and will want more. You offer them more by including them in...

Step six, where you use their **stories about the stories** in broad press releases explaining the growth of the campaign.

By using this tactic you can continuously show that your story is growing in terms of vanity metrics. This will enable you to pitch your story to anyone you want, even the mainstream media.

Why do I call it the **48 hour launch tactic**? Because I spend an insane, caffeine-fuelled 48 hours running it twice around the world, using whatever stories and vanity metrics I have been able to gather in one time zone, in order to launch it in another time zone.

After 48 hours, you will know whether or not you have succeeded with the launch and whether or not you have been able to launch your project. If it hasn't worked, and you don't see a continuous steady growth at this time. Then you need to go back to your core story and start the process all over again.

Remember that you can always use your network if you don't have enough money for bought media. You can either ask them to reach out to journalists and other publishers, or ask them to help you upvote mentions of you on crowdsourcing websites. Please be very selective however, and don't use this tactic unless you feel like your content could pass the strict quality checks that many crowdsourcing platforms run. If you post shit and then try to upvote it, it will blow back at you faster than than you are able to get any kind of value from it.

PSYCHOGRAPHIC TARGETING & NUDGING

I guess I have to talk about the pink elephant in the room, as there are two areas that are growing extensively at the time of writing this book.

Trump just won the election in the US. In part by employing a tactic called "psychographic targeting". The tactic has borrowed a lot of its mechanics from a more traditional form of marketing and behavioral economics called "nudging". The idea is that you first work hard to understand the motivations of a user, and then use that deep understanding to persuade them to do one thing or another.

All of the bubble-bursting tactics above can be performed without any prior knowledge of programming. However, psychographic targeting is really difficult to do without at least some knowledge.

Essentially the method goes as follows.
You catch a user's email address or other similar type of unique identifier. You might have been able to set a cookie on the user when they visited one of your websites, and you know what types of stories they like to share.

You either use the email address or cookie, alongside some knowledge about people who share those kind of stories, to build a profile around that specific user. The profile is built using one or several of the available personality AIs (artificial intelligence) that are available out there.

Each user gets their own profile and a set of messages that will take them on a journey, from where they currently are, to the place where you want them to be taken.

For example, if you want a user to become a passionate 1 for your brand, you would create a user journey where you try to pitch her a set of messages based on her profile. As the profile covers the person's values, morals and other preferences, it is able to adjust messaging, imagery and phrasing to fit every single person who lands on your page.

The page will then be programmed to adjust based on the message that has brought new users there, and subsequently the profiles it collects for those users. This results in a closed system where everyone gets their own, personally tailored and psychographically adjusted content, delivered to them.

Put into the framework of the **conversion formula**, this will surely increase the number of shares of any piece of content, given that the copy will continuously adjust its messaging **Motivation** and most highly perceived **Value Proposition**. Conversion rates will soar.

In order to do this kind of targeting and dynamic page building, you really need to learn some Python, to start connecting some of your CRM-data with Watson's API, and to add some scraped data from each user to what you already got. Boom. In no time at all you'll have your personalised, weaponised messaging system.

Although this is fairly easy to build (honestly!), you should always seek legal advice before you start playing around with deep profiling like this. You should also start small, working in very small segments until you get good at what you are actually trying to do. These kind of automated systems can backfire on you. Computers are simple, and they will operate as if you have given them a clear instruction, even if they haven't fully understood the instruction in the way that you meant it.

We've seen examples of text-based AIs turning into characters of full blown murderers and racists in no time at all. Just because they interpreted their instructions in such a way that they were susceptible to that kind of personality development.

So if you feel uncomfortable with this kind of work, stick with the manual examples at the beginning of this chapter before you move onto the more complex and awesome tools operating at the limits of the digital marketing space.

As with all other things in the book, I will put more links to examples on jesperastrom.com

MORE EXAMPLES
https://goo.gl/YZX6PM

"Without closure, they cannot fully turn their minds to the next step of your journey together."

Maintenance Storing
The Value And Growing

Maintenance Storing The Value And Growing

YOU ARE ABOUT to read the last chapter of this book. As it turns out, this chapter will be more of a "new beginning" than the end of a journey.

One of the things I've learned over the past few years is that I will *never stop learning*. This chapter is aimed at those of you who have a similar mentality. Those of you who want to grow your business or venture gradually over time. When you approach business in this way, there is simply no end to it.

Traditional marketing has been focused on burning a budget, creating something new, and then burning another budget. **The System**, my system, and now your system, instead focuses on storing the equity, network and tangible values that you have built in previous projects, to use for launching upcoming projects.

I call this chapter **Maintenance** because that's what you need to do now. Nothing exciting, nothing new. Simply a process of making sure that you maintain all or part of the value you have built, so that you can reuse it or grow from it.

CELEBRATION

At the end of each of your activations you will have built a lot of excitement and emotion. Do not underestimate these attributes.

People have invested time in your project and they need closure in order to move on. Without closure, they cannot fully turn their minds to the next step of your journey together.

That is why it's super important to celebrate the people who have decided to join your network at the end of every campaign.

The best way of doing this is to use retargeting ads combined with email sendouts. What you do looks a lot like the **celebration** step you read about in the previous chapter, the only difference is that you announce what is happening next.

> *Imagine a situation where you have launched a new line for a specific product. Once the campaign period nears its end, you have the opportunity to communicate to all of those who have purchased the product (meaning the 90's) that there is a new line coming soon. Many brands do this already, but most forget the first part of the messaging. They simply tell people: "Hey, we've got new shit for you to burn your money on." By adding the celebratory prefix to your messaging, you once again remind them of that nice sense of success and completion they felt when they made their previous purchase from you.*

> *Equally, everyone who has blogged about you, needs to know that they did a good job and what it led to. Use all the metrics you can find to reinforce your messaging. Anything from the number of items sold, to the number of views generated from ads, to the number of visitors who came from their respective posts. Tell them that they are meaningful for you, and that you would love to continue the collaboration, and that you are eager to hear where they want you to move next.*

> *By actually doing something with their opinions, perhaps collecting them and publishing them with links back to their social profiles, preferably in a blog post or something similar, you reward them with their preferred currency of **access** to you. You can reinforce that message with something that builds their ego, like words associated with*

professionality, competence or status. This will make it more likely for them to share the post with their friends.

A common practice media publishers use once a year is publishing toplists of people that they have ranked based on some skill or competence. These people love to "humbly" share these lists to their friends in social media. This not only celebrates and adds currency to your relationship with them, but it also attracts other publishers and bloggers to want to join in.

Finally you should focus on your 1's. They are the most important group for you as they will be the people who will start to build your online presence in the future. Now is the time for the ultimate nerd fest. You need to give them insights or behind the scenes access to the results of the campaign that nobody else has access to. Perhaps gather them for a conference, or co-create a video with them by using a live streaming tool. Show them what you do on a day to day basis, open up your factory, or give them access to your CEO during a webinar.

You also need to tell them what you did with their ideas in the last project. If you discarded any of their content you need to tell them why and explain how they can improve for next time. Give them access to the proper production tools and show them how to use your templates. Ask the best ones to provide for the rest of the group and build relationships between them in order to boost creativity.

At best, this can be done in chat groups on LINE, Whatsapp, Slack, or in closed groups on Facebook or Google+. Sometimes you can even do this kind of exercise in a Google Drive doc.

By showing them that you care about them, you will have a much easier time in storing their engagement to use on the next project. The important thing is that you do something. If you are tired, then tell them that you are tired. They are there for you. They love you. And they will be more than willing to help you out by creating a space where you can reward them with your time.

By doing all of these things you be able to will store the value and engagement of your network, which you will be able to build on in future projects.

REDIRECTS

If you have used campaign-specific websites or pages, or perhaps had limited edition products that will now be removed, you need to redirect these pages to other pages that will remain live.

This is something I have a hard time explaining to many marketing professionals. They usually ask me a follow-up question of *where to redirect* these pages. I give them the following answer:

- *If the page* you are redirecting is a product page that will go out of stock, you should redirect it to the closest category page above this page, where other similar products are listed. This will enable users who click the link from other websites to still find something related and useable.
- *If the page* you are redirecting is a landing page for an engagement campaign, then I would write up a blog post about that campaign, explaining its historic context, why it happened and some of its results, then redirect the landing page to that blog post url.
- *If the page* you are redirecting is a through-page to an app or an affiliate product, then I would redirect it to an index page showing related affiliations or applications. Perhaps you have built a new app that is now available, or perhaps you have entered into a new collaboration that would give the user entering your website something of equivalent value.
- *If the page* you are redirecting is none of the above, but it has links pointing to it, I would redirect it to the home page of your website. Or you could redirect to a page where you explain that the previous page has been removed. Make sure you include a search field where the user can type what it is they're looking for. This will become valuable data; perhaps there are things you can put on this landing page that people who come through that link seem to be looking for. This will decrease friction and improve the experience of your user journey, and thus, increase your conversion rates.

A trick you can use for any of the above is to *give the user a gift* because they were looking for something that no longer exists on your website. This is a perfect way to bait for email addresses that can be used for future custom audiences.

> *The user clicks a link on another website and ends up on one of the pages you have redirected to. You have created a form that pops up to all users who enter through this referral to this particular redirect. Above the form*

you write "You were looking for something that no longer exists on our website. In order to help ease some of your disappointment, we are willing to give you this [insert whatever you believe will be valuable]. Enter your email address and we'll send it to you. We will only send this one email if you don't want to know when we launch our next campaign."

Then you add an unchecked box beneath that copy where the user can choose to register for news about new campaigns and projects. OR, perhaps even better, offer them two buttons where one lets them get the offer you're giving them now, and the other gives them the offer + all future offers.

This will work magic for you in collecting user details that can be used to launch future campaigns to your network. The more emails and phone numbers you can collect, the more identifiers you own, and the more relationships you can build. This means that your base reach for the next project, campaign or activation will already be pretty high before you start.

CRM/STORAGE

The next step you should consider is where to store all of your contacts. I like marketing automation solutions where I get to combine email tools with some sort of CRM that tells me about the engagement levels amongst users. I have a list of these tools on jesperastrom.com and will keep it up to date as new tools emerge and existing tools get cheaper.

Some of the things I recommend you to look for in these tools, are multi channel messaging. This is the ability to connect a user to several different accounts and the ability to *message them through* the CRM to email, Facebook and other places at once. This will save you a lot of time.

It's also good if you can work with *automatic tagging* of your contacts, making sure that you'll be able to segment sendouts based on the behavior-type you want to reach (**1-9-90**) and the type of mindset you want to convert (**conservative** or **opportunist**). If you have those functionalities your conversion rates will go up, as you will be able to tailor your content accordingly.

I haven't really found a killer CRM that does everything yet, but I will post whatever it is that I use on my website, so you will be able to do what it is that

I'm suggesting you do, as easily as possible.

CALCULATIONS AND ESTIMATIONS

The next step in the process is to have a look at the time and money you spent on the previous project. This will give you a rough estimate on what results you are able to get for those resources, and what kind of investment it will require in order to be able to produce the next project.

This will give you a few key valuable insights into what you should try to automate, what you should try to build a process around in order to be able to outsource, and what you should stop doing that is not worth your time and effort.

You should tie these calculations to those KPIs you set at the beginning of your project (remember, back in **Chapter 1**) so that you stay true to yourself and your original intentions. If you've changed the KPIs along the way, it is generally just a sign that you didn't perform. In order to improve your work over time, your efficiency and your people skills (which are too important to ignore), you have to stay true to yourself and constantly evaluate what could have been done better. The fact that you didn't perform as well as you thought is great data. Take it. Reflect on it. Learn from it for next time.

If you do this right you will grow as a person as much as you grow your business.

ANALYSIS & INSIGHTS

It's important to start tailoring an analysis framework. I love the ideas from the Lean Analytics project. They suggest that you should use your previous project as your baseline until you have a good benchmark of what is good and bad in terms of results.

You will gradually learn what KPIs are important to follow, and you'll soon have the same problem that everyone in my world has: logging into a hundred tools every day just to get a hold of one metric per tool.

That sounds like a lot of work. So this is probably a good time to start creating *external dashboards*.

An external dashboard will help you fetch single or multiple KPIs from several sources, giving you one dashboard to view them all. This will save you a tremendous amount of time in your next project. You'll be able to just monitor the KPIs in one place follow them in real time as they build over your next project.

Dashboards are also useful if you're working as a consultant or have bosses that need reporting to. I've found them especially helpful as conversation starters. They also have the ability to unite work teams, as the data that is pouring in and the obstacles to reaching success become a sort of *outside enemy* that the team is collectively trying to outsmart.

PREPARATION FOR THE NEXT

Once you have analyzed the data, done your celebrations, and completed your redirects, you now have the opportunity to start building for your next project.

This is the time when you start digging through all the work created by your 1's. You should look through all of the emails you have received, hunting for stories you can use to create a solid narrative of *why you are running your next project*.

Real is always better than fake, and so, if you find a compelling story amongst your existing customers or in your network, then it is much better to *build your future projects around this story*, than it is to come up with some new creative idea on your own.

Yes, of course you probably should add a creative idea to the narrative aswell, but the important lesson to learn about the networked world is that it builds on *anticipation* and *progress*. If you can show that you take care of your network and consumers, it will strengthen the ties across your entire network, rewarding everyone, and not just the person you use for your narrative.

I really don't understand why more brands don't work in this way. I understand that politics, pride and hierarchies can create a mess sometimes. But I don't get why this should always come in between building the relationship with "outsiders" like the brand networks that we've been exploring in this book.

If you can't find a compelling story in your historical data, then use your initial ideas to start prototyping and asking for stories from your 1's. This will give you a *proper* starting point for a real narrative to build into your next project.

This will not only save you time, but it will also give you a wider selection of angles to work from later, when you'll be crafting your **stories about the story**. Since the stories you're harvesting are real, it is highly likely that one or more of them will become **smallest acceptable truths** for other people who become interested in your next project.

Once you have gathered your stories, define your narrative and compare the analytics from the previous project. It's time to set the KPIs and goals for this next project.

AUTOMATION

At this point you will have learned a lot about your users, your processes, and about what works in relation to your product, service or general communications.

This is the point when you can start saving serious amounts of time. Anything that can be automated, should be automated. Be brutal. Your time is the biggest asset you have.

> *Perhaps you receive a frequently asked question about how something works in your previous project. This should be turned into a page on your blog, added as an email in your email automation system, and logged in a list of indexed answers your customer service team can use when they are in touch with your users.*

> *Perhaps you have found out that some journalists open every email that you send and you need to keep them interested in what you do over a long period of time. What you should do is to spend 1hr writing up 52 emails about the topic that interests them, and putting that into an automated chain of emails that is sent to those people once a week.*

Small things like this take time to set them up, but will help you out tremendously once they are in place.

I know only some of you will do this, because most of us are too lazy or have some kind of focus deficiency that makes us *jump on the next train as soon as it enters the station*. But for those of you who are looking for opportunities to save time and have the willpower within you to actually follow through on turning paper-based processes into automated processes... well, you guys are in a good spot to really do some damage.

A full list of automation tools is on jesperastrom.com. If you need any new ones you should simply ask me a question on YouTube or Facebook. My contact details are at the start of the book.

OUTSOURCING

If you can't find an automation tool to do something, you should try to outsource it.

I currently use Upwork as my main outsourcing platform, but that might change a lot depending upon what they do with their fee structure.

My best advice when it comes to outsourcing, is that you should never work with new people on new projects. You have to test people before using them for important work. Always have a side project that you grow over time that can stand the test of a failed delivery.

Some people on these platforms are real scam artists, and you shouldn't feel bad if someone simply takes your money and leaves. The price points are usually so low that you have the ability to fail ten times before you get it right, and you'll still be able to save money. If you have a rigid process. The worst thing you can do is to be in a rush. So if you want to work with outsourcing, either outsource the job to a professional outsourcer that you have a prior relationship with, or spend the time trying several of these online consultants out.

The way I do it is to set up a process and create a workflow using Google Spreadsheets. Then I record a video of me doing *the thing I want the outsourcing partner to do*. I am super detailed in the video and explain every step as though I was explaining it to someone who has never used the internet before.

I don't do that to seem like an asshole, but rather to make sure that *nothing* is lost in translation. A lot of the time you will work with people who don't speak English that well, or who don't know the terminology of your industry. By slowing down the pace, explaining every step as though it was a fantastic innovation, and taking your time to answer any questions (then using those answers to update the film), you will find that you will save a ton of time on this and future projects.

So. My solution for outsourcing. Take the time to test a lot of different people. Use spreadsheets and video to explain the process you want them to deliver. And update your material until everything is clear.

Oh. And one more thing. Check up on deliveries *more* than you find comfortable. Sometimes people don't let you know that they're not going to work on a public holiday, and you'll be stuck with late deliveries as a result. So, don't be afraid when it comes to checking in on their progress, and always demand daily or twice-daily reports on what has been done.

Working this way, you'll earn time on future projects and have more time to focus on the fun stuff that you like doing.

RELAUNCH

Now you've done all the things that you need to do in terms of recovering value from a previous project. Your focus should now be to launch your new project.

Start looking at messaging: who it should be sent to? Look at your narrative and build a schedule. Choose your **activation** principles and consider the **user journeys** and **motivations** that will lead to the **conversions** you want users to make.

Create a matrix where you explain *who* you want to involve and **what currencies** they will be rewarded by. Explain how you will use media purchases in order to guarantee your initial **vanity metrics**, before you have managed to build momentum for your project.

Create example content and get your 1's to start producing prototypes that can enhance it. Then scroll back to page one of this book and start all over.

WHO IS IN YOUR NETWORK NOW...?

DISCLAIMER AND COPYRIGHT